LEARN
EMBROIDERY

Jane Iles

COLLINS

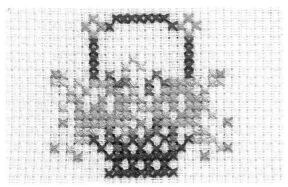

*The author and publishers thank the following
companies which helped with materials for this book:
Coats Domestic Marketing Division for threads and the
place mat design, page 16
Dunlicraft Ltd for DMC threads and for their kind
permission to reproduce the Cross stitch design charts
on pages 24–25
Madeira Threads (UK) Ltd for threads
Needleart House for Paterna Persian wools
Vilene Organisation for non-woven interfacings
C. M. Offray & Son Ltd for ribbons
Thanks also to the following designers and
embroideresses who have contributed to this book:
Beverley Jesset (Stitch samples, page 7, Cross stitch
accessories, page 22)
Vera Read (Long stitch picture, page 10)
Josephine Kane (Arab shirt, page 12)
Lyke Thorpe (T-shirt, page 64)
Betty Laker (Gift cards, page 21)
Jean Crowley (Crewel-work cushion, page 54)
Cluny Johnstone, aged 13, who designed 'Portrait of
Mummy', page 61, and her grandmother Mary Pilcher
who embroidered it.
All other designs by the author*

First published in 1988
by William Collins Sons & Co Ltd
London · Glasgow · Sydney · Auckland · Johannesburg
Reprinted 1989

© Jane Iles 1987

Series Editor Eve Harlow
Designed by Mike Leaman
Photography by Di Lewis
Illustrated by Jill Shipley

Iles, Jane
Learn embroidery. – (Learn a craft)
1. Embroidery
1. Title   II. Series
746.44   TT770

ISBN 0–00–412255–0

Originated in Hong Kong by Bright Arts (HK) Ltd.
Typeset by Nene Phototypesetters Ltd
Printed by Wing King Tong Co. Ltd, Hong Kong

Contents

Introduction

Embroidery, the art of decorating and embellishing fabric with threads and stitches, is an ancient craft that has been developed over the centuries and handed down from generation to generation. Different cultures have each developed their own, distinctive styles and traditional patterns, ranging from the bold and brilliantly colourful work of South America to the delicately coloured and minutely detailed embroidery of the Far East.

Some of the most compelling and beautiful embroidery in the world has been worked by peasants and, sometimes, young children, using very simple tools and materials. Their skills have been developed through patience and practice – and a love of the occupation. So it will be for you. Even if you have never before slipped a needle through fabric, you can learn embroidery.

The projects in this book range from the very simple to designs which are a little more complicated. All are within your range. Stitches are gradually introduced and you will be surprised how few you need to know. Later, you may wish to extend your repertoire of stitches and learn more embroidery techniques.

It is not necessary to be an 'artist' – creativity is in all of us to some extent, whether we have a talent for making gardens, or cooking food, or simply making a comfortable home. Embroidery is for everyone, young and old. You will be learning a craft that women, and men, have been enjoying with deep satisfaction for more than 2000 years. I hope it will give you the same enjoyment and be a pleasure to you, all your life.

Making a Start

One of the biggest setbacks when one is thinking of taking up a new craft is the equipment that has to be bought. Almost any craft is costly at the beginning. This is not so with embroidery. All you really need to start this absorbing, satisfying and rewarding occupation is a piece of fabric, a needle, some thread or yarn and a pair of scissors.

Materials and equipment

If you sew, you will probably find that you have most of the equipment you need in your sewing box.

Fabrics

The fabrics you need to begin embroidery are all around you in your home – dishcloths, handkerchiefs, dish-towels, bed linen and towels, for instance. You do not need to buy expensive embroidery fabrics at the outset. Use what you have around you until the time comes when you want to work a special project.

Needles

Ordinary sewing needles are not really suitable for embroidery work, as the eyes are too small for most threads other than sewing cotton.

Two kinds of embroidery needles are mostly used: tapestry needles and crewel needles. Tapestry needles have large eyes and blunt, rounded tips and are used for working tapisserie yarn and thick threads through linen-type and heavy weave fabrics (as well as canvas). Crewel needles are finer and have pointed tips and large eyes. The patterns in this book usually recommend the needle size required for the thread. If you are ever in doubt as to the size of needle you should be using, remember that the thread should slip into the needle eye easily, and the needle should pass through the fabric easily.

Threads

When you are working a project, it is advisable to buy the type of thread recommended. In this book, you will read about stranded embroidery cotton, Coton à Broder, Coton Perlé or Pearl cotton, soft embroidery cotton, crewel wool and tapisserie wool.

When you are practising stitches, use thread or yarn which you happen to have at hand – even knitting wool. Later, you will be interested to try the different types of yarns and threads available.

Stranded embroidery cotton This comes in a skein and is a smooth, slightly lustrous thread comprised of six loosely twisted strands. The strands are easy to separate (see Fig 6, page 6) and can be used singly or in combinations.

Pearl cotton or Coton Perlé This is a twisted thread with a rich, silky appearance and comes in balls as well as skeins. It comes in three thicknesses: No 8 is very fine, No 5 is slightly thicker, and No 3 is the thickest.

Soft embroidery cotton This is the thickest of all embroidery threads and is similar to crochet or knitting cotton. It is dull, with no sheen.

Coton à Broder This is similar to Coton Perlé, has a shiny finish and is a finely woven thread, usually used for detailed work.

Crewel wool This is a fine, two-ply twisted yarn, popular for embroidery.

Tapisserie wool This is thicker than crewel wool and is primarily used for canvas work where stitches cover the background canvas.

Scissors

For embroidery, you will eventually need to buy a short pair of scissors, about 12.5cm *(5in)* long, with pointed tips. Only use them for embroidery cutting because, if they are used to cut anything like paper, the blades will become blunt and virtually useless for cutting fine fabrics and threads.

Transferring designs to fabric

There are different ways of transferring designs to fabric and most of them are featured in this book.

Direct tracing onto fabric If the embroidery fabric is thin enough for the lines to be seen through it, place the fabric over the design and trace off the lines. Use a coloured crayon as this will wash out in laundering without spoiling the fabric.

Fabric transfer pencils These are sold in various colours and it is a very good idea to have several colours by you

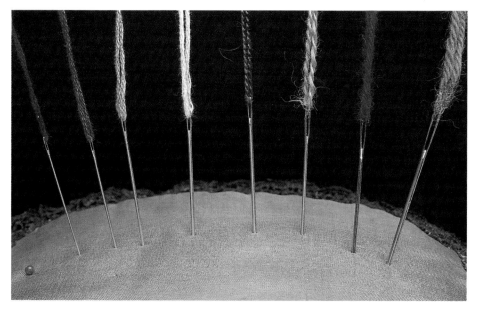

because, if you trace off pattern areas in a colour which is near to the thread colour, there is less likelihood of the lines showing under the stitchery. The most common type is used to draw the design on tracing paper. The paper is then placed face down on fabric and, with the heat of an iron, the design is transferred.

Dressmaker's carbon paper This is liked by some embroiderers but others find that it tends to smudge on the fabric. Place the carbon paper face downwards on the fabric, with the design tracing on top. Draw firmly over the pattern lines with a sharp tool.

Templates These are usually made of card and are made by tracing off the pattern outline and then transferring it onto card. The shape is cut out and then placed on the fabric and drawn around.

Tracing paper and basting This is a time-consuming method but it is often useful when working with thick, rough fabrics. Lay the traced design over the fabric and pin. With basting thread in a contrasting colour to the fabric, work small basting stitches all over the design lines. When completed, gently tear away the paper, leaving the basting threads on the fabric as a guide to embroidery.

Tracing patterns The phrase 'trace the pattern' will appear in several projects in this book. You will need tracing paper, which can be purchased in sheets or in pads from stationers or art shops, or, alternatively, you could use kitchen greaseproof paper. You may find it

necessary to hold the book page to the window, with the tracing paper lightly taped over it, to make the tracing.

Photographic enlargements It is a good idea to enlarge complicated patterns photographically. Many quick-print shops now have photostat machines which will enlarge an image to the size required.

Preparing fabric for embroidery

You will often be recommended to work from the centre of a design outwards to the edges. Also, many commercial pattern charts indicate the middle of a design with arrows set at the sides. You therefore need to mark the middle of your fabric before starting embroidery.

When working with a very fine fabric, measure the width and depth of the fabric with a tape measure. Mark the middle of both long sides and both short sides with pins and then work lines of basting threads between the pins. Where they cross is the middle of the fabric (Fig 4).

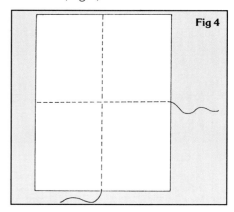

Fig 4 *Marking fabric: work basting stitches horizontally and vertically to find the middle*

When you are working with an evenweave fabric (see Evenweave fabric, page 7), count the threads along one long side and along one short side to locate the centres. Work basting threads across and then down the fabric, starting at these points. The middle is where the threads cross.

Frames and hoops
You will not need an embroidery frame or hoop when you first start embroidery because most of the earlier projects in this book can be worked freely in the hand. However, you will almost certainly

Graph patterns

Many magazines and pattern books feature graph patterns. There are none in this book but you may perhaps want to enlarge a pattern for a particular use, and this is done by making a graph pattern.

The apple motif from page 40 is used as an example.

Trace the motif and then draw a box round it. Divide the box into squares (Fig 1).

Fig 2 shows how the square is enlarged to the size required. Draw a diagonal line through and draw the new, larger box.

Divide the new box into the same number of squares as Fig 1.

From Fig 1, copy the apple onto the new grid by marking in small crosses or dots where the design lines touch the background grid lines.

Join the marks with a line so that the apple is reproduced larger (Fig 3).

You can use the same procedure to reduce the size of a design.

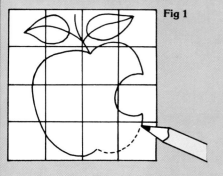

Fig 1 *Enlarging graph patterns: trace the motif and draw a box round. Divide the box into squares*

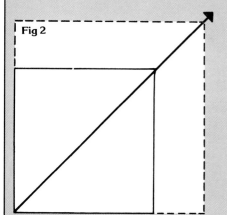

Fig 2 *Draw a square the same size as the box and draw a diagonal line. Draw box to new size*

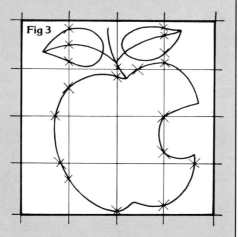

Fig 3 *Divide the new box into same number of squares as Fig 1. Copy motif onto the grid*

want one later.

A circular frame, consisting of two hoops, is used for small pieces of embroidery or on those occasions when the work would be distorted if it were not supported by a frame,

A square or rectangular frame can be made and this will be of great value to you. Use 2 × 2cm (¾ × ¾in) whitewood and cut accurately measured lengths with mitred corners. Fix these together with nails and PVC adhesive. If you prefer you can make a frame where two long sides butt up to two short sides. To use the frame, stretch the fabric over it and fasten with drawing pins or staples. An old picture frame can also be used for a frame, or a stretcher, purchased from an art shop, will do very well.

Handling threads

When you get your new skeins of thread you will see that they are formed so that a strand is loose at one end. Hold the skein as shown in Fig 5 and pull the end. You will find that the thread pulls

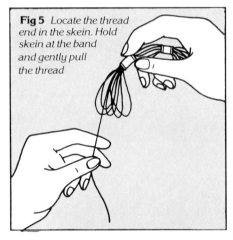

Fig 5 *Locate the thread end in the skein. Hold skein at the band and gently pull the thread*

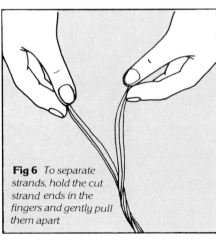

Fig 6 *To separate strands, hold the cut strand ends in the fingers and gently pull them apart*

out easily without tangling.

To separate one or two strands, cut the thread from the skein and hold it as shown in Fig 6 and gently pull the threads apart.

Starting and finishing thread

Although in some cases, it is acceptable to tie a knot in the thread end, you should try not to get into the habit of always doing this because it will spoil the look of your embroidery on the wrong side.

To make a neat start, push the needle through the fabric about 5cm (2in) from where you will begin stitching, leaving a 'tail' on the right side. Then bring the needle through at the point you intend to begin stitching. When this thread end is finished, take the thread to the wrong side and darn the end into

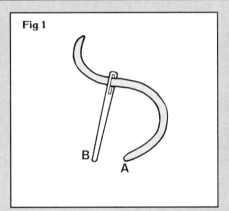

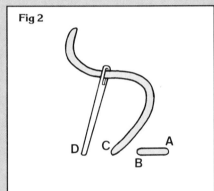

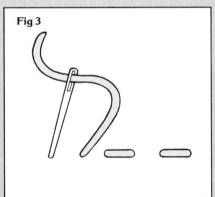

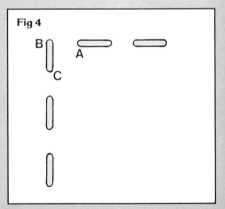

Running stitch

1. Tie a small knot on the thread end. Bring the needle through from the wrong side at A and insert the needle at B, a short distance away (Fig 1).
2. Bring the needle out at C and insert it at D. Two stitches have now been worked (Fig 2).
3. Continue in the same way (Fig 3).

embroidery already worked.

Then thread the 'tail' into the needle, take this through, and darn in the end.

When cutting thread, never cut more than 45cm (18in). This is about the most you can comfortably handle.

When working motifs, it is best to finish off the thread end and start again on the next motif. It looks untidy when stitches are taken across the back of the work.

The first stitch

The first stitch in embroidery is a small, straight stitch called Running stitch. The needle and thread pass into the fabric and then come out a distance away, and then continue, passing in and out of the fabric, leaving stitches on the

Running stitches should all be of the same length but the spaces between the stitches can vary, as long as you are constant in spacing throughout the piece of work.

Turning corners

Having reached the corner (Fig 4), bring the needle out at A and insert it at B, then bring the needle out at C, and a square corner is made.

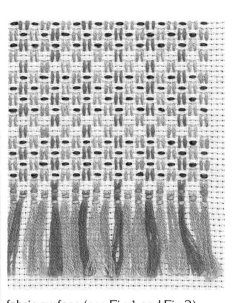

fabric surface (see Fig 1 and Fig 2).

Running stitch can be quite small, covering only two or three threads of fabric – or it can be longer, from 6mm–12mm ($^1/_4$–$^1/_2$in) long. It is a very simple stitch to do but, worked in bright threads and with the stitches varying in length, it can be very decorative.

You can use patterns of Running stitches to decorate all kinds of items – children's and babies' clothes, lingerie and nightwear, jeans and jackets and, for the home, tablecloths, dishcloths, place mats, cushions and curtains. Running stitches worked through curtain net look very individual, worked in embroidery thread of the same colour or in a contrasting shade.

Pattern darning

Pattern darning is a technique used in many parts of the world. It has been worked by embroiderers as a decoration for garments, robes and furnishings for more than 2000 years.

In principle, stitches are worked through an evenweave fabric to make patterns (see pictures). They can be worked close together, so that the background fabric is entirely covered, or the fabric can be part of the colour scheme.

Stitches can be worked horizontally (like Running stitch), vertically, or they can slant diagonally.

To practice pattern darning, you will need a piece of openweave embroidery fabric called binca which has a defined square weave, making it easy to position stitches correctly. If this is not available, you can use a piece of hessian or sacking (burlap).

Top left: *Pattern darning stitches worked decoratively, with thread ends left in a fringe.*
Above: *Pattern darning and Straight stitches worked together*

Evenweave fabric

When fabric is woven, the vertical threads (called the warp) are held on the loom. The weft threads are woven through the warp threads. Most fabrics used for embroidery are in a plain weave where the weft goes alternately over and under the warp threads (see diagram). When both the warp and weft threads are of the same weight the fabric is called evenweave fabric and you will find references to this in different projects in this book. Evenweave fabric is used for counted thread stitches (such as Cross stitch) where fabric threads are counted with the needle tip to position the stitch correctly and to ensure that stitches are of the correct size.

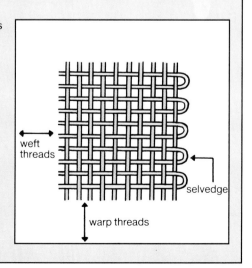

Straight Stitch

Straight stitch can be a counted thread stitch or a free-style stitch, depending on the fabric and the design. Both forms are in this chapter. You are shown how to work Peruvian-style cushions on dishcloth cotton, embroider a shirt with a 2000 year-old Arab pattern, work a set of place mats, create daisy-sprigged curtains and embroider a garden – all with Straight stitches.

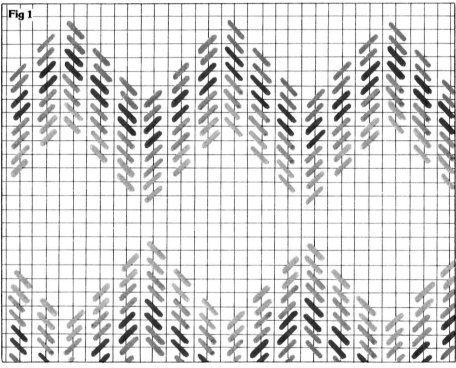

Fig 1 *Pattern for the zigzag cushion with part of an adjoining zigzag. Follow the colour sequence*

Fig 2 *One quarter of the tasselled cushion pattern; The black arrows indicate the middle of the design*

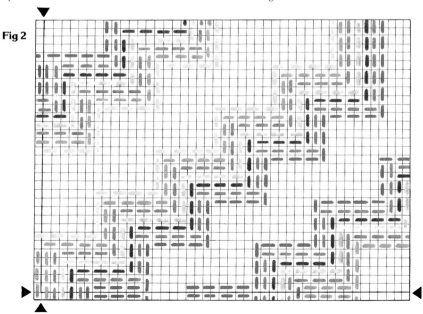

Peruvian-style cushions

Soft cotton dishcloths with an open weave are used to make these bright cushions. Inspiration for the patterning is taken from the bold, geometric designs that have decorated Peruvian peasant clothes for hundreds of years.

Materials required
For both cushions
4 cotton dishcloths with an open weave, approximately 33cm *(13in)* square
70cm *(28in)* of 91cm *(36in)*-wide cotton fabric
Double knitting yarns, 1 ball each of emerald green, jade green, royal blue, bright pink (for the zigzag cushion), plus bright red, turquoise and yellow (for the tasselled cushion)
Tapestry needle, size 18
White sewing thread
Two 30cm *(12in)*-square cushion pads

Preparation
Cut four 33cm *(13in)* squares from the cotton fabric. Take two of the dishcloths and attach each of them to a cotton square, pinning round the edges. Baste all round and remove the pins. Machine-stitch all round, 6mm *(¹⁄₄in)* from the edge. Remove the basting stitches.

Working the embroidery
Work the embroidery on the two remaining dishcloths.

Fig 1 is the pattern for the zigzag cushion and shows a complete zigzag, with part of the adjoining zigzag. Repeat this pattern across the dishcloth following the colour sequence as shown in the picture (pink, royal blue, jade green, emerald green).

Fig 2 is one-quarter of the tasselled cushion pattern. The black arrows indicate the middle of the design. Fig 3 shows how the four quarters are worked to make up the whole pattern. Measure the dishcloth to find the middle and mark this with basting threads (see Fig 4, page 5 for the technique).

To work this project, you may tie a knot in the yarn end, although it is better to take a double stitch around the edge of the fabric to secure the end.

Starting at the edge, pass the needle

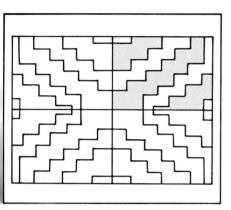

Fig 3 *Repeat the pattern Fig 2 as shown to make the complete tasselled cushion*

smoothly through the fabric, working over and under threads as shown in the charts. Do not pull tightly on the stitches but ensure that they lie smoothly on the fabric surface. Work each line of the design with one length of yarn.

Leave the yarn ends hanging at the edges or finish them, without pulling up, with a double stitch through the fabric edge.

Making the cushion

When the embroidery is completed, mount the dishcloth fabric on a piece of cotton fabric as you did for the cushion back. Place the front and back together, right sides facing, and pin and baste on three sides. Machine-stitch, taking a 12mm (½in) seam. Remove the basting threads and turn the cover to the right side. Insert the cushion pad and close the open seam with hand-sewing. Work both cushions in the same way.

Finishing

For the tasselled cushion, make sixteen tassels from the remaining yarn, following the instructions given. Sew four to each corner, as shown in the picture.

For the zigzag cushion, cut 4m of each of the remaining yarn colours and make a twisted cord, following the instructions are given here. Apply the cord to the cushion edges as follows: double the cord and form a loop. Sew the loop to one corner of the cushion. Continue sewing the cord to the four sides of the cushion, making and sewing loops on the two facing corners. On the last corner, tie the cord ends in a bow and sew to secure. Knot the cord ends about 10cm (4in) from the bow and trim to make tasselled ends.

Twisted cords and tassels

Cords Cut wool yarn to 2½–3 times the finished length of cord required. Hold the ends firmly in each hand and twist the yarn. Continue twisting until the yarn coils upon itself. Allow the yarn to twist, then take the middle in one hand and the ends in the other and pull gently so that the cord straightens. Knot the ends together (Fig 1).

Tassels Cut several 10cm (4in) lengths of wool yarn. Fold in half to make a bunch. Tie a piece of yarn round the bunch as shown, knotting the ends. Trim the ends to the length desired (Fig 2).

Fig 1

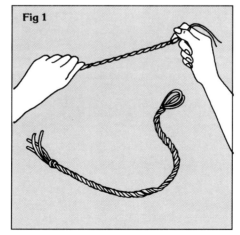

Fig 2

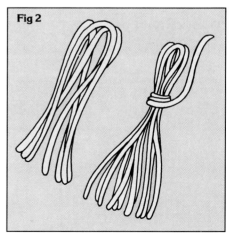

Long stitch pictures

The technique of picture-making with long stitches originated in Scandinavia and it has become a popular type of needlework, especially for beginners and young people.

It is very easy to do and the work grows quickly so that the picture is soon finished.

The method is only suitable for pictures because the long threads lie on

Straight stitch

Straight stitch can be worked vertically, horizontally or diagonally and the stitch length varies to fit the shape of the area being worked. Stitches are worked close together so that the fabric background is covered and does not show between the stitches.

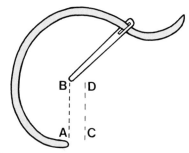

Fig 1 *Vertically: work the stitch in the same way, bringing the thread through at A and inserting it at B. Bring the needle through at C and insert it at D to make the second stitch*

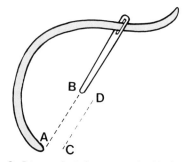

Fig 2 *Diagonal stitches are worked in the same way. When working freestyle, make sure all stitches lie at the same angle*

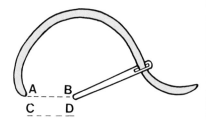

Fig 3 *Horizontally: bring the needle through at A and insert the needle at B. To make the second stitch, bring the needle through at C and insert it at D.*

the surface of the fabric and, if used for items such as cushions, the threads would catch in wear.

Two pictures are given here for you to work and practise the stitch. The tree picture is the simplest, with the background fabric forming part of the design. The country landscape is more difficult, with small areas to work,

Tall tree
Materials required
27 × 23cm *(10¾ × 9in)* piece of Aida fabric with 14 threads to 2.5cm *(1in)*
DMC Tapisserie wool as follows:
1 skein each of 7314 blue, 7771 bright green, 7364 mid-green, 7367 dark green, 7541 bottle green, 7402 light green. 7337 grey-green, 7619 brown, small amount of white
Tapestry needle, size 22

Preparation
Trace the design from the picture and transfer it to the fabric using an embroidery transfer pencil.

Working the design
Follow the picture for the direction of the stitches and colours. All the stitches are long stitches, set either horizontally or vertically. The only exception is the pair of birds which are worked with two diagonal Straight stitches.

Country landscape
Materials required
25 × 30cm *(10 × 12in)* piece of Hardanger fabric with 9 threads to 1cm *(22 threads to 1in)*
Paterna Persian yarn as follows: 1 skein each of 553 ice blue, 555 pale ice blue, 261 cream, 522 teal blue, 713

Fig 1 *Trace-off pattern for the Country Landscape. Follow the colour picture for the direction of stitches*

mustard, 614 pale hunter green, 664 pale pine green, 612 mid-hunter green, 433 mid-chocolate brown, 403 mid-fawn brown, 405 pale fawn brown, 406 beige
Fabric transfer pencil and tracing paper (or dressmaker's carbon paper)
Tapestry needle, size 22

Preparation

Trace the pattern (Fig 1). Trace over the lines on the wrong side of the paper with the fabric transfer pencil. Following the manufacturer's instructions, transfer the picture to the fabric. (If dressmaker's carbon paper is being used, follow the technique described on page 4).

Working the design

An embroidery hoop will make the work easier and will also help to prevent the yarn being pulled too tightly. If neither a hoop nor an old frame is available then great care must be taken to see that all the stitches lie smoothly on the fabric

without puckering.

Follow the picture for the direction of the long stitches. Note, for instance, that the ploughed fields have stitches lying diagonally (see illustration and the picture).

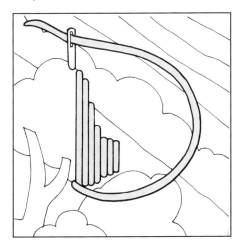

Fig 2 *Here vertical Straight stitches are worked to different lengths, close together, to fill the design area*

Finishing both pictures

When the embroidery is completed, cut a piece of stiff card and lace the picture as described on page 27. Alternatively, tape the fabric edges to the back of the card with adhesive tape.

Fig 3 *Work Straight stitches diagonally for the ploughed fields, vertically for the grass, hedges and foliage with tree branches in horizontal stitches*

Arab shirt

The shirt in the picture is made of cream evenweave fabric embroidered with a motif of triangles on the neckline and round the sleeves. The design was taken from an old Middle Eastern robe embroidery and Arab women have been working similar patterns on their garments for more than 2000 years.

Stitches based on Straight stitches are used mostly in Middle Eastern embroideries and brilliantly colourful designs are achieved.

Materials required

To work 1 neckline motif and 2 sleeve borders
DMC stranded embroidery cotton as
  follows: 2 skeins each of 919 brown,

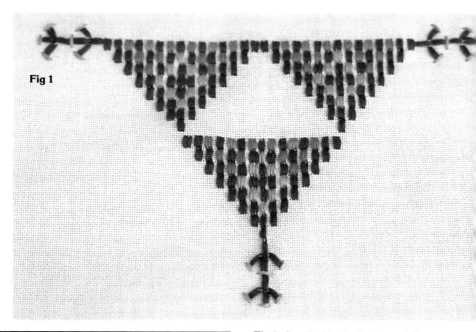

Fig 1

Fig 1 *Detail of the Arab shirt neckline showing the arrangement of the Straight stitch pattern. Each stitch is worked vertically over 6 threads of fabric and there are 3 stitches to a block. Leave 3 threads between each block*

  892 coral, 807 blue, 972 yellow, 905 green, 976 tan
Tapestry needle, size 24

Working the design

Measure and mark the middle of the fabric (refer to Fig 4, page 5 for the technique).

The colour picture (Fig 1) is a detail of the neckline motif and you can work the embroidery from this, matching thread colours and remembering that stitches are worked vertically over 6 threads of fabric in blocks of 3 stitches, set 3 threads apart.

Fig 2 is a section of the sleeve border. The blocks each have 2 stitches in them, worked over 6 threads of fabric and set 3 threads apart. The border has bands of Square stitch and working instructions for this are given in Fig 3.

Straight stitch on evenweave fabric

On evenweave fabric, fabric threads are counted to position the stitches correctly.
1. Bring the needle through at A and insert it 6 threads above at B. Then, bring the needle through at C (1 thread to the left of A) and insert it at D, 6 threads above and to the left of B. Work the third stitch of the block in the same way (E–F).
2. To work the next block, take the needle 3 threads to the left and bring it out at G ready to make G–H, the first stitch of the next block.

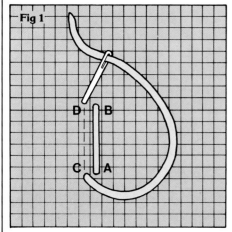

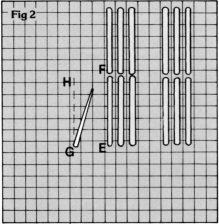

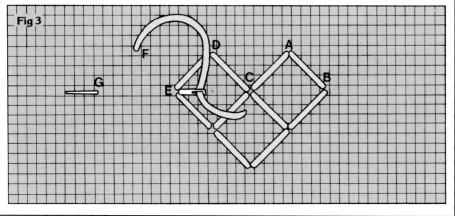

Fig 3 *Square stitch: The stitch is worked in two stages. In the first stage, the needle is brought through at A, inserted at B four threads down and four to the right, and brought out at C, eight threads to the left and level with B. Insert the needle in the same place as A and bring it out at D, eight threads to the left and level with A. Insert the needle at C again and bring it out at E, eight threads to the left and level with C. Insert the needle at D again and bring it out at F. Insert at E and bring out at G and so on. This makes a series of half squares. Work the other half of the squares in the same way, reversing the stitch.*

Fig 2 *Section of the sleeve border pattern. Here, blocks have 2 Straight stitches in them, worked over 6 threads of fabric and 3 threads apart. Work Square stitch above and below the Straight stitch pattern (see Fig 3)*

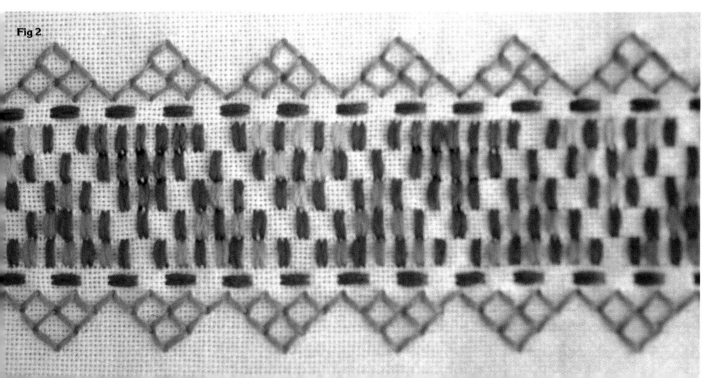

Fig 2

Daisy-print curtains

Straight stitches can also be worked on finely-woven fabrics, such as the polyester lawn used for the curtains in the picture. Here, straight stitches are worked so that they radiate from a central point and the finished effect is like a daisy.

Daisies can be worked to any size and can have just eight petals as shown or have a number of petals close together. The embroidered daisies are worked over painted spots of fabric paint (see Fig 4).

Materials required
White polyester lawn fabric, sufficient to make two curtains
Fabric paints in red, white, blue and yellow (or fabric crayons in pastel colours)
Paintbrush, items for printing 'blocks' (corks, bottles, bottle caps, etc)
Stranded embroidery threads in pink, pale blue and yellow
Crewel needle, size 7
White sewing thread

Preparation
Wash, dry and iron the curtain fabric. Spread the fabric over clean newspaper and weight it at the corners so that it does not shift during printing.

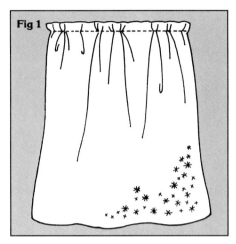

Fig 1 *Follow this arrangement of daisies or work a random design of your own*

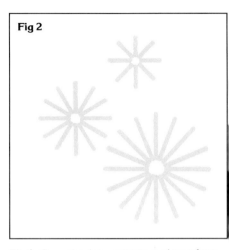

Fig 2 *Trace the daisy patterns and transfer to the fabric using the direct tracing method*

Mix the fabric paints according to the manufacturer's instructions.

Fig 1 shows the arrangement of the daisies on the curtain pictured. Follow this arrangement for your own curtains or work in a random fashion, printing colour spots to your own design.

Brush a little colour onto your chosen printing 'block' and press it firmly on the fabric. Spots can overlap if you like. Print all the spots and leave the fabric to dry. Print two matching curtains.

To fix the colour spots, spread clean cotton fabric over the printing and iron for 1–2 minutes with the iron at a very hot setting. Wash, dry and iron the printed curtains.

Transferring the pattern
Trace the daisies from Fig 2 and transfer them to the fabric, positioning daisies over the colour spots (see Fig 4). Any of the transferring methods described on page 5 can be used but the direct tracing method is recommended for this project.

Working the design
The embroidery is worked with three strands of embroidery thread in the needle.

Divide a 38cm *(15in)* length as described on page 6.

Tie a single knot on the thread end. Work the daisies as shown in Fig 1 to

Straight stitch daisies

In this project, Straight stitch is worked as a free-style stitch to form daisies. Stitches are worked over the transferred design lines.
1. Bring the needle through to the right

side of the middle of the daisy at A. Insert the needle at B (Fig 1).
2. Bring the needle through at A again and insert it at C (Fig 2).
3. Two petals of the daisy have now

been worked. Continue bringing the needle through at A and work each of the petals in turn (Fig 3). Finish the thread end on the wrong side at A with a tiny back stitch.

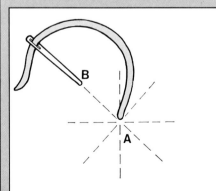

Fig 1 *Bring the needle through to the right side at A and insert it at B*

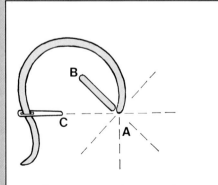

Fig 2 *Bring the needle through at A again, ready to make the next stitch. Insert the needle at C to make the second petal*

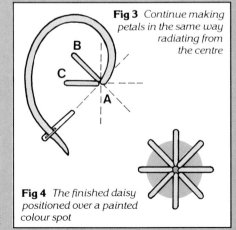

Fig 3 *Continue making petals in the same way radiating from the centre*

Fig 4 *The finished daisy positioned over a painted colour spot*

Fig 3, matching the thread colour to the printed circles. You may vary the length of the petals if you desire – it will help to give freedom to the finished embroidery.

Finish each daisy off as it is worked. Do not be tempted to work from one daisy to the next without finishing off the yarn because this will produce an untidy look on the wrong side – and both sides of a curtain show.

Work two matching curtains.

Lining embroidered curtains

If you prefer to line your curtains, use the same white polyester fabric. Cut the lining to the same size as the curtain, then trim 4cm *(1 1/2in)* from the long edges of the lining. Place the curtain and lining together, right sides facing, and pin and baste the long edges together. Machine-stitch.

Re-fold the curtain so that the lining is centrally positioned on the curtain. Press. Turn up the hem and machine-stitch. Finish the top edge with a casing or with curtain tape.

Place mats

In this project, Straight stitches are worked close together to make Satin stitch. Cross stitches and Back stitches are also used in this design. The instructions for working these stitches are given on pages 22 and 37

Materials required

For 2 place mats 40 × 28cm (16 × 11in)
2 pieces of 50 × 38cm *(20 × 15in)* evenweave embroidery fabric with 29 threads to 2.5cm *(1in)*
Anchor stranded embroidery cotton as follows: 3 skeins of 850 marine blue; 2 skeins each of 311 tangerine, 361 light golden tan, 362 golden tan, and 848 light marine blue; 1 skein each of 313 tangerine, 889 brown
Tapestry needles, sizes 20 and 24

Preparation

Mark the centre of both pieces of fabric across the narrow width with basting stitches (see page 5, Fig 4 for the technique). Fig 1 is the chart for one complete motif of the border design. The background lines represent threads of fabric and the heavier lines represent stitches.

The open arrow is the centre of the border and should coincide with the line of basting thread. Fig 2 is the chart for the corner motif. The key for stitches and colours for both charts is given.

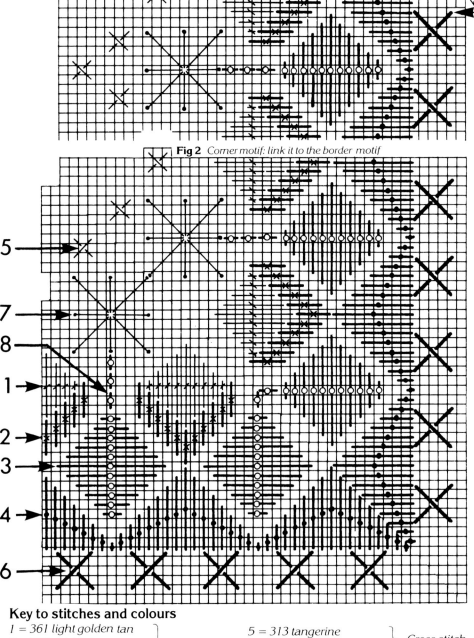

Fig 1 *One complete motif of the border. Begin at the black arrow*

Fig 2 *Corner motif: link it to the border motif*

Key to stitches and colours

1 = 361 light golden tan
2 = 362 golden tan
3 = 848 light marine blue   Satin stitch
4 = 850 marine blue

5 = 313 tangerine
6 = 889 brown   Cross stitch
7 = 311 tangerine   Straight stitch
8 = 848 light marine blue   Back stitch

Working the embroidery

Four strands of thread are used for the embroidery with the exception of those stitches worked in 850 marine blue, where six strands are used. Use the larger needle for this.

With the long side of fabric towards you and starting at the point marked with the black arrow on Fig 1, commence stitchery following the chart and the colour key. Begin the border 5cm (2in) from the edge of fabric.

Work the motif 9 times to the left and then work the corner motif (Fig 2). Turn the fabric and work the Fig 1 motif 11 times, then work the corner motif (Fig 2) and continue working Fig 1 motifs up to the basting lines. This completes half of the place mat. Complete the other half in the same way.

Make two matching place mats.

Finishing

Press the embroidery on the wrong side. Trim the fabric to within 6cm (2³⁄₈in) of the embroidery, then turn a 2.5cm (1in) hem, mitring the corners. Slipstitch the hem.

Secret garden

The secret garden picture is in effect a painting done with threads. Long and Short and Straight stitches are worked at different angles, in grouped masses and individually, to catch the light and to interpret the foliage, grasses and flowers of a lush, overgrown garden.

The stitches completely cover the fabric and here you have the opportunity of adding some of your own ideas to the project when placing the stitches and choosing colour tones.

Materials required
40 × 80cm (16 × 32in) piece of white cotton fabric

Fig 1 *Trace-off pattern for the Secret Garden picture. The broken line is a guide for cutting the mount*

35 × 45cm (14 × 18in) piece of pale-coloured printed cotton fabric
Embroidery hoop 25cm (10in) diameter
Tracing paper
Felt-tipped pen
Anchor stranded embroidery cotton as follows: 1 skein each of 35 red, 316 orange, 375 soft brown, 347 brick, 117 pale violet blue, 158 very pale blue, 160 pale blue, 216 mid-sage, 225 emerald, 206 mid-forest green, 264 pale olive, 255 grass green
Crewel needle size 7
28 × 38cm (11 × 15in) piece of strong card
23 × 33cm (9 × 13in) piece of strong card
Clear adhesive
Masking or adhesive tape

Preparation
Fold the white cotton fabric in half and place it in the embroidery hoop, making sure the fabric is taut and evenly stretched.

From Fig 1, trace the outlines of the garden. Use a fine felt-tipped pen as this will dry and, unlike pencil, will not smudge on the fabric. Pin the traced design to the fabric and transfer the pattern using the basting thread technique (refer to page 5).

Working the embroidery
Use three strands of embroidery thread throughout.

With this type of project, it does not matter where you begin and it is in fact preferable for you to be working several areas at the same time. Think of your embroidery as a painting, where it is better to work the whole subject rather than isolated shapes which will eventually fit together.

The stitches that are used are freely arranged and you do not have to count threads or make sure that they are identically placed. You are creating a garden and if, for example, you want to work some extra orange Cross stitches because you like the effect they create, then this is good. (Refer to page 22 for Cross stitch). You are learning to recognise, select and reject design areas as well as to work new stitches.

The sky is worked in two shades of pale blue thread which is built up in Long and Short stitches (see Fig 1–Fig 5, page 20) which fit together and curve around the top of the design.

rounded bloom shapes. Work the branches in the darker brown thread building up the slightly jagged and angular shapes with lines of several single stitches.

The foliage around the edges of the garden is freely built up with several clumps of long Straight stitches using the three stronger shades of green so that they look like grassy plants.

Working the flowers

Once you have worked all the foliage, you will have quite a large area of green. To break this up, you now add the flowers. The orange flowers are tiny Cross stitches worked randomly so that they look as if they are scattered over the tops of the grassy patches (refer to page 22).

The red and violet-coloured flowers are similarly worked to give this scattered effect but are made by grouping sets of two or three small stitches together, placing them in different directions as you did with the foliage of the trees.

Finally, the grassy patch is worked in the two pale shades of green with long Straight stitches placed horizontally across the garden to give the effect of shadows across a lawn. Work a few tiny clumps of brighter green stems and orange or violet flowers on the lawn to add interest to this smooth, flat area.

Finishing

Once the embroidery is completed, remove the fabric from the hoop. If necessary, press it on the wrong side to remove any creases and to 'emboss' the depth of the stitchery on the right side.

Place the embroidery right side down on a clean, flat surface and centre the smaller piece of card on it. Stretch fabric over the edges of the card, pulling it with the fingers and working from the centres of opposite sides to give a smooth, tight effect on the right side of the embroidery. Cut across the corners to remove excess fabric which would be bulky when folded. Glue the turnings to the card with clear adhesive and then tape the fabric edges.

To make the fabric mount for the picture, use the arched dotted line on the pattern (Fig 1). Centre the original tracing on the larger piece of the card and cut out the shape with a sharp crafts knife.

With Straight stitches, work small clumps of grass randomly spaced over the printed cotton fabric to link it with the embroidery. As the clumps are well-

The trees are worked to give a completely different effect. The three stronger shades of green have been used in patches to give areas of dense leafy colour beyond the brick wall. The actual stitch construction is simple. Work clusters of about four closely grouped Straight stitches.

The clusters are then randomly scattered so that they are not facing the same way (see picture). This emphasizes the slight sheen of the stranded cotton as it picks up and reflects light. The larger patches of green can be 'lifted' by scattering a few isolated stitches of a different green on the leafy clusters or, alternatively, working some brown Straight stitches to represent the tree branches.

The wall is worked entirely in the brick colour 347, building up small oblong shapes with the stitches laying horizontally across the wall, leaving a small gap of bare fabric between each brick. Remember to stagger the positioning of the bricks from one row to the next and, as the wall becomes hidden by the garden foliage, you will have to fill in the small gaps where the bricks can still be seen with groups of smaller horizontal stitches.

The foliage of the large rose bush with the red blooms is worked in a similar way to that of the trees, but with a less dense effect, so that the wall can be seen between the leaves. The blooms are then built up with clusters of Straight stitches positioned to give the

spaced, each clump should be worked separately, starting and finishing off thread ends neatly so that there is no risk of the green thread showing through the fabric. Keep the tension even.

Press the fabric on the wrong side and place it right side down on a flat surface. Place the larger piece of card on it, centring it, and stretch the fabric onto the card. Cut out the centre

section of the fabric, leaving 1cm (³⁄₈in) all round for turnings.

Clip into the curved upper edge and also into the lower corners so that the fabric can be smoothly stretched.

Fold the turnings onto the card, gluing it down and then taping the edges.

Finally, glue and tape the embroidered panel to the back of the window mount.

Long and Short stitch

1. Bring the thread through at A and insert it at B. (Fig 1). To make the next, longer stitch, bring the needle through at C and insert it at D, close beside B (Fig 2).
2. To make a short stitch, bring the needle through at E and insert it at F close beside D (Fig 3).
3. To work the second row, bring the needle through at G and insert it at H between 2 long stitches (Fig 4). The third row is worked as the second with stitches fitting into the second row (Fig 5).

Greetings cards in stitchery

Greetings cards and 'thank you' cards, embroidered especially for the occasion, are always received with delight and they are fun to do. The cards in the pictures are all worked on a Christmas theme but every kind of occasion is an opportunity for working small, simple pieces of embroidery for cards.

Ready-made card mounts can be purchased from most needlework shops and are available in different sizes and styles. Mounts can also be made at home, using thin card or construction paper.

Making card mounts
The size of the envelope will decide the dimensions of the card. Make the card about 3mm (¹⁄₈in) smaller all round so that it slips in to the envelope easily.

Round or oval-shaped windows are not recommended as these are difficult to cut cleanly.
1. Having decided the finished size of the card, draw the shape three times, edges touching, as shown in Fig 1. Measure and draw the 'window' on section 2. Using a sharp crafts knife, cut out the 'window'.
2. Using a large, blunt-tipped needle and a metal edged ruler, score along

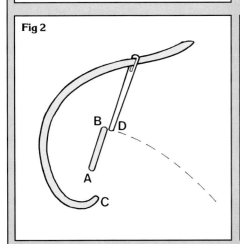

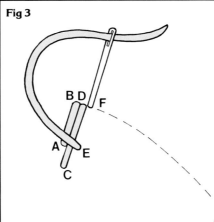

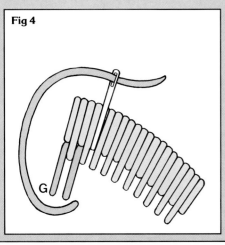

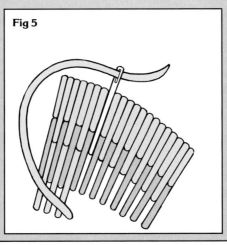

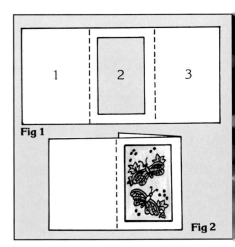

Fig 1 *Draw the card shape three times, edges touching as shown. Cut a window in the centre section 2*

Fig 2 *After mounting the embroidery on the wrong side of section 3, fold 3 onto 2*

the fold lines on the inside of the card. Fold on the scored lines.

3. Trim the finished embroidery so that it is a little smaller than the card. Spread a little clear adhesive, very thinly, on the edges of section 3, on the wrong side. Position the embroidery right side up and press on the edges to fix it in place. Leave to dry.

4. Spread a little clear adhesive, very thinly, round the window, keeping it at least 3mm (¹/₈in) from the edges. Press section 3 onto section 2. Fig 2.

Motifs and designs

Motifs used for small cards should be simple and the effect will be more pleasing if stitches are kept to two or three kinds. Suitable motifs can be found in embroidery pattern books or you can trace designs from books, magazines, gift papers, etc. Some of the motifs given for Cross stitch on pages 24–25 are suitable for gift cards.

Patterns for the Christmas cards in the picture are not given but similar designs can be worked from the following details.

Snowflake

Size of motif, 5 × 5cm (2 × 2in)
Fabric Blue evenweave linen, 28 threads to 2.5cm (1in).
Threads White stranded embroidery cotton, silver embroidery thread.
Stitch Cross stitch (page 22) over two threads of fabric.

Sequin tree

Size of motif, 6 × 4cm (2¹/₄ × 1¹/₂in)
Fabric Finely woven dark green polyester/cotton.
Threads and materials Black stranded

embroidery cotton, silver embroidery thread, 26 gold sequins, 1 gold sequin star, 17 small green glass beads, 9 small red glass beads.
Stitches Straight stitch (page 10) and oversewing. To work the design, bring the needle through from the wrong side of fabric, pass it through a sequin, then thread on a bead and pass the needle back through the sequin. Proceed immediately to the next sequin without fastening off the thread.

Candle glow

Size of motif, 6.5 × 3cm (2¹/₂ × 1¹/₄in)
Fabric Finely woven dark blue polyester/cotton.
Threads Stranded embroidery cotton in orange, peach and old gold, and silver

embroidery thread.
Stitches Outline the candle in silver thread with machine-stitching or by hand using Stem stitch (page 56). Work the flame in old gold in Stem stitch. Decorate the candle with rows of stitchery: Stem stitch, Chain stitch (page 42), Fly stitch (page 59) and couched Straight stitches (page 53)

Add groups of three French knots (page 53).

Silver tree

Size of motif, 9 × 4cm (3¹/₂ × 1¹/₂in)
Fabric Finely woven dark green polyester/cotton.
Threads and materials Silver embroidery thread, pearlised sequins.
Stitches Work the tree shape with machine stitches or by hand using Stem stitch (page 56) or Backstitch (page 37). Sew on the sequins with silver thread. Work a small double Cross stitch (page 22) at the tree top.

Three candles

Size of motif, 4cm (1¹/₂in) square
Fabric White evenweave embroidery linen, 24 threads to 2.5cm (1in).
Threads Stranded embroidery cotton in red, green and gold embroidery thread.
Stitches Use Cross stitch (page 22) for the candles, Straight stitch (page 10) for the candle flames and Fly stitch (page 59) for the tree branches.

Cross Stitch

Cross stitch is popular with beginners because it is a very easy stitch to work and there are many designs available in pattern books which use it. In this chapter you are given a library of motifs so that you can make pretty accessories or design your own sampler. You will then feel ready to work a violet herb pillow, make bright Christmas decorations or stitch a 'Bear in bed' nightwear bag for a child.

Small accessories

The accessories pictured are all decorated with Cross stitch and most of them can be worked in only a few hours. Some of the motifs are given as charts on pages 24–25.

Framed baby name Worked on Aida cloth with 11 holes to 2.5cm *(1in)*. Threads are DMC stranded embroidery threads as follows: 776 pink, 334 blue, 913 green, 554 mauve, 445 yellow. (Chart for letters Fig 1.)

Redcurrants Worked on Aida linen with 14 holes to 2.5cm *(1in)*. Threads are DMC stranded embroidery cotton as follows: 349 red, 350 light red, 904 green, 907 light green, 221 brown-red. (Chart: Fig 2.)

Key ring Worked on Aida linen with 14 holes to 2.5cm *(1in)*. Threads are DMC stranded embroidery cotton as follows: 794 mid-blue, 956 bright pink, 957 mid-pink, 818 light pink, 745 yellow, 703 green, 310 black. Two strands used throughout. (Chart: Fig 3.)

Duck picture Worked on Aida linen with 14 holes to 2.5cm *(1in)*. Threads are DMC stranded embroidery cotton as follows: 973 yellow, 322 blue, 701 green, 666 red, white. The chart is Fig 4. To achieve the size, stitches are worked over 2 squares of the fabric.

Porcelain box top Worked on Aida linen with 14 holes to 2.5cm *(1in)*. Threads are DMC stranded embroidery cotton as follows: 793 blue, 794 light blue, 895 dark green, 3347 mid-green, 745 yellow, 335 dark pink, 963 light pink.

Two strands used throughout. (Chart: Fig 5.)

Gardener's diary Worked on Aida linen with 14 holes to 2.5cm *(1in)*. Threads are DMC stranded embroidery cotton as follows: 322 dark blue, 3325 light blue, 813 blue-grey, 318 grey, 922 orange, 402 light orange, 445 yellow, 890 dark green, 988 mid-green, 945 flesh. (Chart: Fig 6.)

Hairband Worked on embroidery riband 5cm *(2in)*–wide. Threads are DMC stranded embroidery cotton as follows: 890 dark green, 352 dark coral, 754 light coral, white. Work over two squares of the fabric. (Chart: Fig 7, border pattern.)

Cushion Worked on Aida linen with 14 holes to 2.5cm *(1in)*. Threads are DMC stranded embroidery cotton as follows: 798 blue, 957 mid-pink, 905 green. (Chart: Fig 8.)

Cherries jam pot cover Worked on Aida linen with 14 holes to 2.5cm *(1in)*. Threads are DMC stranded embroidery cotton as follows: 349 dark red, 352 light red, 350 medium red, 986 dark green, 988 mid-green, 472 light green. (Chart: Fig 9.)

Paperweight Worked on Aida linen with 14 holes to 2.5cm *(1in)*. Threads are DMC stranded embroidery cotton as follows: pink 893, mid-green 988, yellow 744. (Chart: Fig 10.)

Pincushion Worked on pink evenweave linen with 22 holes to 2.5cm *(1in)*. Threads are DMC stranded embroidery cotton as follows: 554 light mauve, 327 dark mauve, 550 purple, 445 yellow, 966 light green, 318 grey, 776 pink, 3350 dark pink. (Chart: Fig 11.)

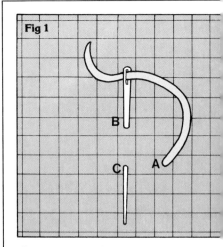

Fig 1

Cross stitch

Cross stitch is a counted thread stitch and is worked on evenweave fabric. It can be worked from right to left or left to right, as you wish. The upper stitch of the cross can slant in either direction but it must lie in the same direction throughout a piece of embroidery.

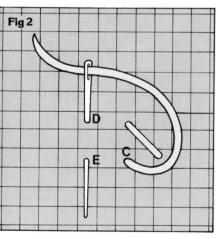

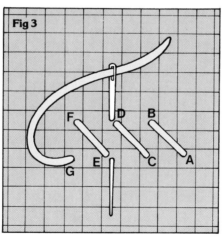

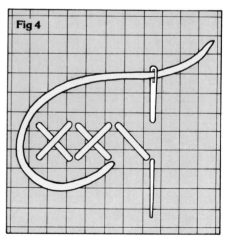

When working Cross stitch, it is a good idea to try always to go down through holes which have a stitch already in them and come up through empty holes.
1. Bring the needle through at A and insert it at B, two threads up and two threads to the left. Bring the needle

through at C to complete half the Cross stitch (Fig 1).
2. From C, take the needle to D, two threads up and two threads to the left, then bring the needle through at E, to make half of the 2nd stitch (Fig 2).
3. Continue in the same way E–F.

To complete the cross, having brought the thread through at G, insert the needle at D (two threads up and two to the right), and bring it out at E (two threads down) Fig 3.
4. Continue in the same way completing the Cross stitches.

Sampler motifs

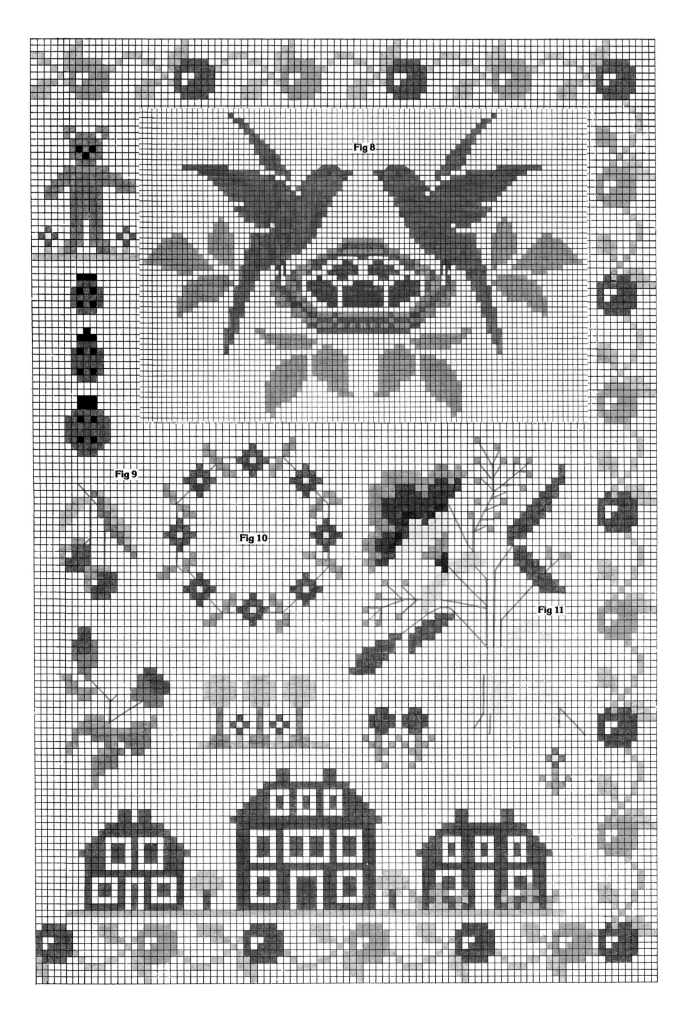

Fig 8

Fig 9

Fig 10

Fig 11

First sampler

In the days before printed patterns, samplers were a means of recording embroidery designs and motifs and embroiderers would use them to try out stitches, colours and threads before using the designs in the final piece of work.

By the eighteenth century, samplers had become an accepted method of teaching young girls to do needlework and charming examples of their work can still be found today.

Although samplers are still popular as a form of needlework, few embroiderers bother to make their own designs nowadays, although it is by no means difficult to do. Samplers are an ideal way of recording family events and occasions – weddings, christenings, births, graduations and anniversaries – and, as such, make perfect gifts.

The sampler pictured is made up of children's motifs and a alphabet, and these motifs, with others, are given on pages 24–25. Using these motifs, you will be able to design your own sampler.

If a special motif you want is not given, it is possible to make your own from a picture or drawing from a book.

Planning a sampler

Decide the overall dimensions first. You may, for instance, already have a frame you would like to use. Draw the area of the sampler on graph paper. Remember that every square represents one stitch and not a thread or hole.

Cross stitches can be worked over a single vertical and horizontal thread or over two or more threads. Count the number of squares on one long side and one short side of your chart and then count the number of stitches that will be worked on your fabric, to make sure that you have the size of sampler you require.

Select or design your motifs and plan any words or lettering. Copy these onto your graph paper chart, colouring them in the thread colours you intend using.

You may prefer to copy larger motifs onto pieces of graph paper and cut them out so that you can experiment with different arrangements.

When planning a border, start in the middle of the sides and work towards the corners. The design may have to be adjusted to go round the corners neatly.

Preparing the fabric

Having made sure that your charted sampler is the size you want, count threads and outline the area for embroidery with basting threads. Count threads to find the middle vertically and horizontally and mark with basting threads.

Cut out the fabric at least 10cm *(4in)* from the basted outline.

You may wish to mount the fabric in an embroidery frame for working, but you can also work the fabric freely in your hand.

Using a Cross stitch chart

Count squares and mark the vertical and horizontal middle of the chart. It is a good idea to begin either with the lettering or the largest motif. Follow the basted lines and the marks on the chart to ensure that the embroidery is centred on the fabric.

You may find it helps to concentrate your eye on the motif you are working by cutting a hole in a piece of paper and pinning this over the motif, thus blocking out surrounding designs.

Have several needles threaded with

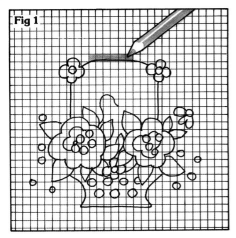 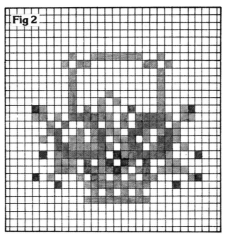 

Designing Cross stitch motifs

You will need some squared graph paper and coloured pencils or felt-tipped pens.

Trace the picture or drawing on tracing paper. Rub soft pencil over the back of the tracing and then draw over on the right side onto graph paper.

Each square of the graph paper is going to be a Cross stitch. Colour the squares following the traced outline. Sometimes the line will go through the middle of a square. This does not matter as long as the motif keeps its general

shape. Choose the best squares to achieve the effect (Fig 1).

Fig 2 shows the basket motif coloured and ready for working the embroidery. The picture shows the basket worked in stranded embroidery cotton.

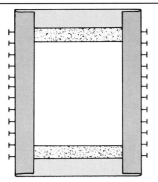 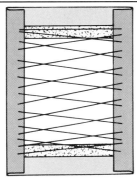 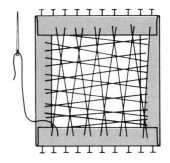

Fig 1 *Fold and stretch fabric edges to the wrong side and insert pins to secure*

Fig 2 *Lace edges together with long stitches as shown and then remove the pins*

Fig 3 *Fold top and bottom edges to the wrong side, pin and lace the edges*

Displaying and mounting embroidery

Embroidery must be mounted on card to display it properly, especially before framing. To do this, cut a piece of thick card to the desired size. If the fabric is thin and semi-transparent, it is a good idea to pad the card with a piece of non-woven interfacing. Cut it to the same size as the embroidery fabric.

Press the embroidery carefully on the wrong side and spread it right side down

on a flat surface. Lay the non-woven interfacing on top, matching edges. Lay the card on the fabric, centring it. Fold the two side edges onto the card, inserting dressmaker's pins into the edges as you work (Fig 1).

Thread a needle with a long length of thread and tie a small knot in one end. Pass the needle through the fabric at one end and work lacing stitches back and

fourth across the mount as shown in Fig 2.

While the lacing is being worked, continually stretch the fabric so that it is as smooth as possible. Remove the pins as you lace.

Fold in the other sides and pin, as before, and then work lacing to hold the fabric edges stretching the fabric smoothly (Fig 3).

Remove the pins.

different colours by you so that you can change colours quickly. When working a solid block of stitches the needle should, if possible, be brought to the front of the work through an unworked hole in the ground fabric, and go down through holes where stitches have already been worked. This will produce

a neat and even area of stitchery, as it prevents the possibility of previously worked stitches being split by the needle point.

Remember that it is important to work all the Cross stitches identically with the uppermost stitches facing the same way throughout.

Finishing

When the embroidery is completed, carefully unpick the basting threads. The finished sampler should be lightly pressed on the wrong side, stretched and laced over a piece of thick card ready for framing.

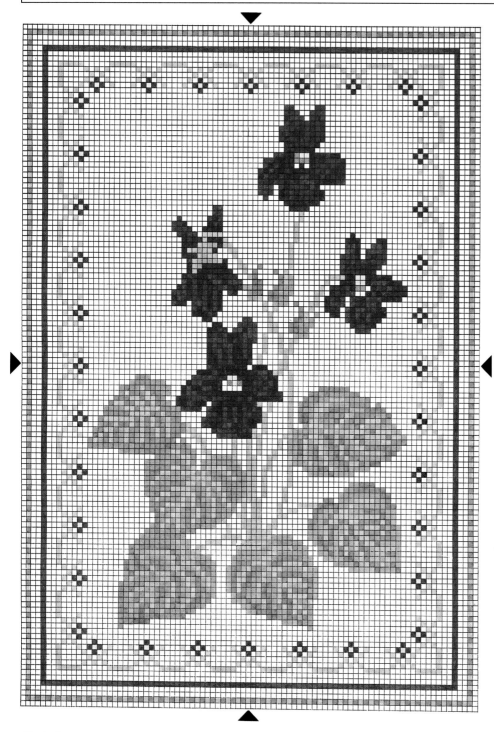

Fig 1 *Chart for the wild violet design. Match the colours here to the embroidery threads, following the key. Work each Cross stitch over 2 horizontal and 2 vertical threads*

Violet pillow key

- ☐ = M367 mid-green
- ☐ = M989 light green
- ☐ = M907 bright green
- ☐ = M740 orange
- ☐ = M743 yellow
- ☐ = white
- ☐ = M208 violet
- ☐ = M554 pale violet

Wild violet pillow

This Cross stitch project demonstrates how a small design or motif can be enlarged on graph paper to make a bigger design.

The wild violet design was adapted from a drawing on a small seed packet. The first stage was to trace the drawing and then transfer it onto a graph paper with very small squares. The outline was then copied onto paper with larger squares, thus enlarging the original drawing.

The chart was then coloured, copying the original seed packet colours. Each square of the chart represents one Cross stitch worked over two vertical and two horizontal threads.

If preferred, the original tracing could have been enlarged photographically and the graph paper chart made as described on page 27 (Fig 1 and Fig 2).

Materials required
Finished size 35 × 28cm (14 × 11in)
43 × 35cm (17 × 14in) piece of white evenweave fabric with 12 threads to 1cm (27 threads to 1in)
38 × 30cm (15 × 12in) piece of white fabric for backing the pillow
Madeira embroidery floss as follows: 1 skein each of M208 violet, M554 pale violet, M740 orange, M743 yellow gold, M989 light green, M367 mid-green, M907 bright green; white 1 skein of Anchor Pearl cotton No. 5, colour 97 mauve (for edging cord)
Crewel needle size 7.
Coloured basting thread, sewing threads in white and mauve
Soft cushion pad

Sachet of lavender, pot pourrie or fragrant herbs (optional)

Preparation
Press the fabric to remove any creases and mount it in an embroidery frame. (If you prefer, you can work the embroidery freely in your hand.)

Baste the horizontal and vertical centre guidelines, using coloured sewing thread. (Refer to Fig 4, page 5).

Working the design
Three strands of embroidery floss are used throughout.

It is a good idea to begin working near the centre of the design to ensure that your embroidery is accurately placed on the fabric.

Following the chart (Fig 1) work the embroidery in Cross stitch (see page 22) working each cross over 2 vertical and 2 horizontal threads. Make sure that

all the stitches are worked with the uppermost stitch facing the same way throughout.

Making the pillow
When the embroidery is completed, carefully unpick the basting threads. Press the fabric very lightly on the wrong side.
1. With the embroidered area centred, trim away the excess fabric to 38 × 30cm (15 × 12in). With right sides together, place the pillow front and back together. Pin, baste and machine-stitch on two short sides and one long side, taking a 15mm (⅝in) seam.
2. Trim the corner points diagonally and turn the pillow to the right side. Push out the corners with a blunt pencil.
3. Place the cushion pad inside the embroidered case and turn in the raw edges of the opening. Hand-sew the edges to close.

Finishing

Using the mauve Pearl cotton, make a twisted cord to go all round the pillow plus 30cm (12in), (see Fig 1, page 9). Sew the cord to the pillow using matching sewing thread, sewing on the seam line. Begin and end at the bottom right hand corner. Tie the cord ends into a bow. To neaten the ends, tie a knot near to each end and then carefully fray out the loose threads to give a tasselled effect. If you prefer, make tassells as shown in Fig 2 page 9.

Making a herb pillow

This kind of pillow makes a charming accessory if a sachet of fragrant herbs or lavender is put into the cushion pad.

Carefully unpick part of a seam and push the sachet into the middle of the pad. Close the seam with hand-sewing.

Symbol charts

Some artist's materials shops and draughtsmen's suppliers stock sheets of clear acetate printed with squared grids of different sizes. These are extremely useful for making counted thread embroidery charts.

Simply place the grid over the drawing or photograph you wish to interpret into stitches Copy the design onto squared paper.

Draw the design in chart form on the tracing paper, using symbols to represent the various colours.

Here is a simple symbol/colour guide you may like to use. This covers only twelve colours but you can invent other symbols for more colours.

⊡	red	◥	brown
◰	blue	◼	black
⊠	green	◧	pink
◤	yellow	◩	cream
◫	orange	⊟	crimson
☐	white	✳	navy blue

Christmas snowflakes

Soft, embroidered ornaments for the Christmas tree are very popular in Scandinavian countries and it is an idea worth copying. The small snowflake ornaments in the picture are made on Binca fabric and take only a few hours to work.

The design given has two variations. in the first, the snowflake is simply worked in white Cross stitches on red fabric and then outlined with Back stitches using green thread.

In the second variation, an embroidery technique called Assisi work is used. In this, the motif is left unworked while the surrounding fabric is filled with Cross stitches. Traditionally, the design is then outlined with Back stitches, which can also be used for additional detail on the motif.

Assisi embroidery is said to have been evolved by the nuns in the Convent of St Francis in Assisi, Umbria, in central Italy. Local records show that, as early as the fourteenth century AD, this type of Cross stitch embroidery was being worked in designs abstracted from wood carvings.

Materials required

For each decoration, finished size 7cm (2¾in) square
2 pieces each 9cm (3½in)-square of red binca fabric
Contrasting basting thread
Anchor Pearl cotton as follows: 1 skein each 01 white, 225 green (only part used)
Tapestry needle, size 24
Red sewing thread
38cm (15in) piece of 3mm (⅛in)-wide green ribbon (optional)

Preparation

Count the holes along two sides of one fabric square to find the middle and mark the fabric with lines of basting threads vertically and horizontally.

Working the embroidery

The middle of the design (Fig 1) is indicated with black arrows on the edges. This corresponds with the middle of your fabric, marked with basting threads.

Begin the embroidery in the middle

of the design and work outwards.

After the Cross stitches have been completed, work green Back stitches (see page 37) around the snowflake, setting stitches the space of one Cross stitch away (Fig 2).

Assisi snowflake

Prepare the fabric in the same way and work from the middle of the design (Fig 1)

Green Back stitches can then be worked on the inside edge of the Cross-stitched background.

Making up the ornament

Carefully remove basting threads. Place the embroidered square to an unworked square, right sides out and pin. Fold the ribbon as shown in Fig 4 and tuck it between the fabric squares at one corner. Baste to hold the ribbon in place.

Using red sewing thread, machine-stitch around the four sides of the ornament, stitching along the line of holes just outside the embroidery. Fray the threads away up to the line of stitching. Trim to a neat fringe (see picture). Remove basting threads.

If preferred, thread loops could be sewn to one corner of the ornament.

Two-sided ornaments

If preferred, the ornaments could be embroidered on both sides – one side worked in the first way and the other in the Assisi variation. Other colour schemes could also be worked: green and red threads on white binca, or white and gold threads on blue binca, for example.

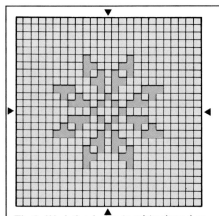

Fig 1 *Work the design in white thread on coloured fabric or in coloured thread on white fabric. Each square represents one Cross stitch*

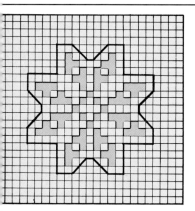

Fig 2 *Outline the finished motif with green Back stitches (see page 37), setting stitches the space of one Cross stitch away*

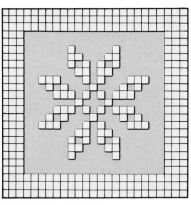

Fig 3 *To work Assisi snowflakes, work the background to the motif in Cross stitches, leaving the motif as unworked fabric. Outline the motif with Back stitches if you prefer*

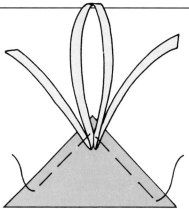

Fig 4 *To make the ribbon hanger, fold the ribbon in half then bring the ends up as shown. Sew the hanger loop between fabric layers at one corner*

Bear in bed

This nightwear bag is made of binca – a type of evenweave fabric with holes which enables stitches to be worked easily and accurately. Binca is an ideal fabric for practising Cross stitch because it has a square weave.

The bag has a drawstring top and is large enough to take a child's long nightgown or a pair of pyjamas. It would also make a shoe bag.

Materials required

Finished size 43 × 31cm (17 × 12½in)
2 pieces each 50 × 35cm *(20 × 14in)* of white binca fabric
Anchor soft embroidery cotton as follows: 1 skein each of 290 yellow, 132 mid-blue, 229 emerald green, 238 light green, 335 bright red, 403 black, 352 brown; 2 skeins of 129 pale blue
Tapestry needle, size 24
Basting thread
White sewing thread
1m *(1⅛yd)* of white piping cord

Preparation

On one piece of fabric, count the holes along one long side and one short side to find the middle of each. Work basting threads across and down the fabric. The middle of the fabric where the basting threads cross corresponds with the middle of the Cross stitch chart (Fig 1), indicated by the black arrows.

This embroidery can be worked freely in the hand or the fabric can be mounted in a frame.

Working the design

Working from the chart and following the colour key, work the design in Cross stitch (see page 22). Start in the middle and work outwards to the border, making sure that the top stitch of each cross faces in the same direction.

Making the bag

Press any creases from the fabric. Place the embroidered front and the bag back together, right sides facing. Pin and baste on the long sides and along the bottom.

Starting 3cm *(1¼in)* from the top edge, machine-stitch all round, taking a 15mm *(⅝in)* seam. Remove the basting threads.

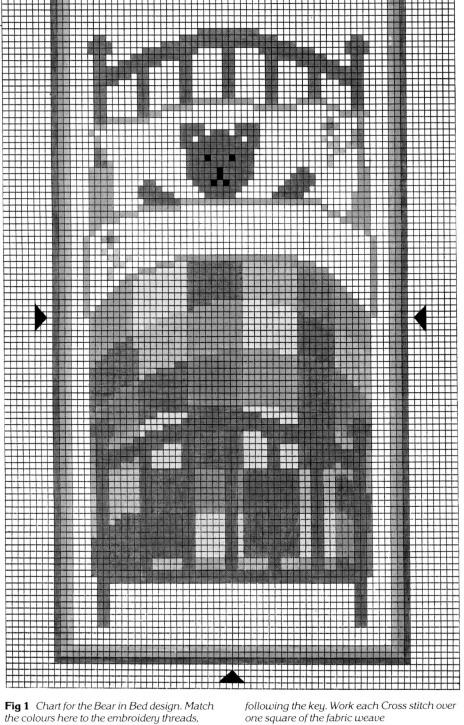

Fig 1 *Chart for the Bear in Bed design. Match the colours here to the embroidery threads, following the key. Work each Cross stitch over one square of the fabric weave*

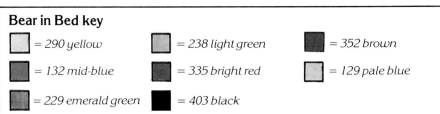

Bear in Bed key

= 290 yellow	= 238 light green	= 352 brown
= 132 mid-blue	= 335 bright red	= 129 pale blue
= 229 emerald green	= 403 black	

Trim the bottom corners diagonally and turn to the right side. Turn a narrow hem on the top edges and then turn and baste a deeper hem to make a casing for the cord. Machine-stitch the casing hem.

Finishing

Fasten a safety pin to the end of the cord and slip it through the casing. Knot the cord ends together. Pull the cord loop out from the other side of the bag to make two loops (see picture).

Ideas for the design

The 'Bear in bed' design can be used to make other needlework furnishings. If the design is worked on a soft, evenweave fabric with each Cross stitch 6mm (¼in) across, the design would enlarge to approximately 67 × 35cm (26½ × 14in) and this would make a charming embroidery for a bed cover.

Worked in rug wool on rug canvas, the same design makes a matching bedside rug. By tracing the pattern (Fig 1) and enlarging it photographically, the 'Bear in bed' could also be used for an appliqué project.

Back Stitch

Back stitch is a very useful stitch and is used primarily for outlining. It can also be used in massed rows to fill an area and, on evenweave fabric, complex linear patterns can be built up. In this chapter, Back stitch is used to embroider curtain ties with a butterfly and ivy design and the same theme is used to work a quilted cushion.

Butterfly tieback and cushion

Only Back stitch is used for the embroidery, worked along the design lines. The stems of the foliage appear slightly thicker than the other lines (see picture). This is achieved by working two lines of Back stitches in two shades of green thread.

Tieback

Materials required

For one tieback 3 pieces of firm white cotton fabric 60 × 30cm *(24 × 12in)*
Anchor stranded embroidery cotton as follows: 1 skein each of 205 jade green, 241 pale jade green, 337 pale russet, 339 mid-russet. 110 mid-violet: 2 skeins each of 253 pale green, 95 pale mauve, 305 mid-gold
Crewel needle, size 5
130cm *(52in)* of bright green narrow cord
Sewing thread to match cord
2 small plastic rings

Preparation

Trace the pattern Fig 1 on pages 36 37, matching the design lines as indicated and re-trace, to produce a complete pattern.

Spread the pattern on a flat surface and place a piece of the cotton fabric on top. Smooth the fabric and hold in place at the edges with strips of adhesive tape.

Trace over the design lines with a fabric transfer pencil (or washable crayon). Remove the fabric with the design traced upon it and place over a second piece of the cotton fabric.

Smooth the layers together and then baste with soft basting thread, starting in the middle and working out to the edges.

Place the mounted fabric in an embroidery hoop, stretching it carefully until the fabric is quite taut. You will only be able to fit part of the design in the hoop to start with, and will need to remove and reposition the fabric several times to complete the design.

Working the embroidery

Six strands of embroidery cotton are used together throughout the embroidery to give a bold and well-defined line.

Choose any area to begin embroidery and follow the colour key for the correct thread to use. Work even Back stitches (see Fig 1–Fig 4 page 37) along all the lines of the design. It may be necessary to work smaller Back stitches at corners or when working small shapes.

Work the butterfly wing outlines before filling in the veins. Work the ivy leaves and continue the stitching into the stems, thickening them slightly by working a second line alongside using a different shade of green.

When the embroidery is completed, remove it from the frame and unpick the basting threads. Press the fabric on the wrong side very lightly, to encourage the stitchery to appear 'embossed' on the right side.

Making the tieback

Trim the excess fabric away up to the cutting line. Place the embroidery right side down on a piece of the cotton fabric. Pin and baste the layers together along the seam line, 1cm (⅜in) inside the cutting line.

Machine-stitch on the seam line, leaving a gap on a curved edge approximately 10cm (4in) long.

Trim away the surplus fabric and snip into the seam allowance on the curves. Turn the tieback to the right side and press very gently, if necessary.

Close the open seam with tiny-hand sewing stitches.

Make a second tieback in the same way.

Sew the green cord around the edges of the tieback, starting and ending on one of the short sides.

Making covered rings

Using pale green thread 253, work Buttonhole stitch (see page 48) over the rings until the plastic is covered. Tie the thread ends together (Fig 1).

Sew the covered rings to the middle of each of the tieback's short side.

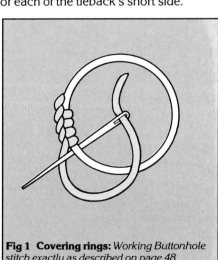

Fig 1 Covering rings: *Working Buttonhole stitch exactly as described on page 48 to cover a ring*

Butterfly motif

The butterfly motif (Fig 2) is a simple linear design and is ideal for practising Back stitch. It can be used to decorate the corner of a traycloth or on a place mat and napkin set. Several butterflies could be worked along the edges of a cotton curtain, or randomly placed on a fabric blind.

Butterflies are also delightful motifs for children's clothes, particularly if a few daisies are added to the design (refer to page 14).

Butterfly tieback and quilted cushion key

- = 253 pale green
- = 241 pale jade green
- = 205 jade green
- = 305 mid-gold
- = 337 pale russet
- = 339 mid-russet
- = 95 pale mauve
- = 110 mid-violet

Fig 1 Curtain tie pattern: *Trace the pattern piece on folded paper: re-trace to obtain a complete pattern. Join the two segments where they are broken across the middle of the page*

Fig 3 *Trace the motif and use it for decorating table linens, or work several in a random pattern on curtains or a blind*

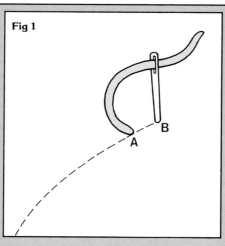

Fig 1

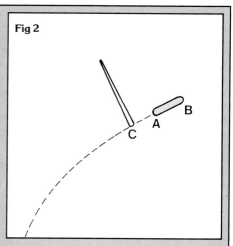

Fig 2

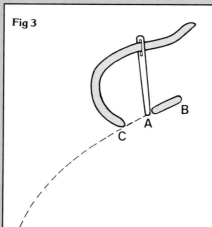

Fig 3

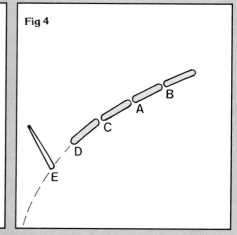

Fig 4

Back stitch

In working Back stitch, it is important that every stitch is of exactly the same length and this takes practice to achieve. It is worth trying several lines of Back stitches on scraps of fabric until a smooth and even line of embroidery is worked and then you will be ready to try the butterfly motif.

1. Bring the needle through on the design line at A and insert the needle at B (Fig 1).

2. Bring the needle through at C (exactly the stitch length of A–B) in front of A (Fig 2).

3. Re-insert the needle at A again, in exactly the same hole previously made (Fig 3).

4. Bring the needle through at D (making sure the distance between C–D is the same length as the previous stitches), and insert it at C, in the same hole (Fig 4). Continue making stitches in the same way.

Quilted cushion

The pretty quilted cushion in the picture on page 34 has the same Butterfly and ivy pattern as the curtain tieback.

Back stitch is used for the quilting and the use of fabric transfer crayons adds delicate colour to the effect.

Materials required

80cm *(32in)* of 152cm *(60in)*-wide white polyester cotton

50cm *(20in)* square of medium-weight polyester wadding

35cm *(14in)*-diameter circular cushion pad

Anchor stranded embroidery cotton as follows: 1 skein each of 337 pale russet, 305 mid-gold, 110 mid-violet, 241 pale jade green, 205 jade green

Crewel needle, size 7

White sewing thread

50cm *(20in)*-square piece of tracing paper

Fabric transfer crayons

45cm *(18in)*-square wooden embroidery frame (for mounting the fabric)

Preparation

Spread out the white cotton fabric and measure and cut off two strips each measuring 15cm *(6in)* by the width of the fabric (152cm *(60in)*).

Put these aside for the cushion frill.

Measure and cut the remaining fabric into three squares, each 50cm *(20in)*-square. Put one of these aside for the cushion back. Stretch one of the remaining squares over the wooden frame, aligning the sides of the frame with the straight grain of fabric. This is important to prevent the fabric becoming distorted.

On the sheet of tracing paper, draw a circle with a radius of 17cm *(6¾in)*. This will be the seam line of the finished cushion. (If you prefer, you can draw the circle by tracing the quarter segment of the cushion pattern given (Fig 1), moving the paper and re-tracing the segments to obtain the complete circle.) Place the tracing paper over the pattern (Fig 1), matching the seam line with the broken line. Using fabric transfer crayons, lightly colour in the design. As each quarter-segment is coloured, re-align the tracing paper

until the complete pattern is obtained.

Be careful not to smudge the crayonned surface as the tracing paper is moved, as this will show on the fabric later. Try to use the crayons smoothly so that an even spread of colour is achieved.

Press the second piece of fabric to remove any creases. Place the crayonned paper face down on the fabric, centring it. Press very carefully with an iron to transfer and fix the design on the fabric. (Follow the manufacturer's instructions for the heat of the iron.)

Great care must be taken not to move the paper while pressing as this will blur and distort the image.

Place the wadding over the stretched fabric in the frame and spread the printed fabric on top, right side up. Make sure that the straight grain of the printed fabric aligns with the sides of the frame.

Pin the three layers together at the sides of the frame. To do this, press the layers down with one hand and smooth the top fabric and wadding towards the side of the frame with the other. Insert

the pins. Repeat this process on the opposite side of the frame and then work the two remaining sides. The wadding should be firmly 'sandwiched' between the layers of fabric.

Working the embroidery

Three strands of embroidery cotton are used throughout the embroidery.

Following the instructions for working Back stitch on page 37, work even Back stitches on all the lines of the design, through all the thicknesses of fabric. The colour key for the cushion is the same as for the tieback (see page 36

Work the inner parts of the design first and then work outwards towards the edges. Work round the leaves and butterflies before adding details of veins, antennae, etc.

The lines of Back stitches will 'pinch' the wadding around the wings and leaves so that they appear to be padded and 'embossed'.

When all the embroidery is completed, baste around the seam line using white sewing thread. (Use the paper pattern as a guide.) Remove the quilted fabric from the frame.

Fig 1 Quilted butterfly cushion: *One-quarter of the round cushion pattern. Trace the shape on a square piece of paper then move the paper and re-trace the shape, joining design lines at the edges so that a complete circular pattern is obtained*

Cut out 1cm *(³⁄₈in)* from the seam line.

Making the cushion

Join the two strips of fabric on the short ends to make a ring of fabric. Fold along the length, matching the raw edges and with wrong sides together. Work two rows of gathering stitches through the raw edges. Carefully draw up the gathering threads to fit the frill along the seam line of the cushion.

Fasten off the gathering threads with a small Back stitch and then pin the frill to the right side of the cushion along the seam line, matching raw edges. Baste with small stitches so that the gathers are held evenly. Machine-stitch through the gathers leaving a 15cm *(6in)* gap in the seam. Remove the basting thread.

Place the remaining piece of fabric on the cushion, right sides together so that the frill lies to the middle. Pin and baste the layers together on the stitched

seam line. Machine-stitch on the same line of stitching as before leaving a 15cm *(6in)* gap in the seam. Remove the basting threads. Trim away the surplus fabric. If you prefer, the raw edges of the seam allowance can be oversewn together to neaten them. Turn the cushion cover to the right side.

Insert the cushion pad through the gap in the seam. Fold in the raw edges and hand-sew with small stitches, using white sewing thread.

Chain Stitch

During the previous chapters, you have worked Straight stitches in a variety of ways and you are now ready to learn a more complicated stitch – Chain stitch. This is one of the many loop stitches and it can be used in different ways: as an outlining stitch, as a filling stitch and in flower-like groups. In this chapter, you are shown how to work simple apple motifs on a place mat, tray cloth and on children's play clothes, and then how to create a Forget-me-not tablecloth and napkins.

Apple place mat

Place mats and tray cloths are a good way of displaying your embroidery expertise – and an opportunity for practising new stitches. Linen-weave place mats can be purchased ready-made in many department stores and, decorated with a simple embroidery motif, become a personalised home furnishing.

The apple (Fig 1) is designed as a practice piece for Chain stitch and it should take a beginner just over an hour to complete.

Materials required
Yellow linen weave place mat
Piece of thin cardboard for a template
Embroidery transfer pencil
DMC Coton Perlé No. 5, 1 skein 704 green
Crewel needle, size 5

Preparation
Trace the apple outline and leaves from Fig 1 ignoring the 'bite' shape for this project. Rub soft pencil over the wrong side of the tracing. Lay the tracing on thin card and draw over the lines with a sharp pencil. Cut out the apple shape and the leaf shapes.

Using templates
On the place mat pictured, the apple is positioned 3.5cm *(1¼in)* from the bottom hem edge and 4.5cm *(1¾in)* from the right-hand hem edge. Place the apple template on the fabric and hold it down with the fingers. Draw round with an embroidery transfer pencil. Draw in the short stalk free hand.

Then place the leaf templates against the stem on the right and left of the stalk and draw round it.

Working the embroidery
This embroidery can be worked freely in the hand without a hoop if preferred.

Using the Coton Perlé and following the diagrams (Fig 1–Fig 4, page 42), work Chain stitch round the apple outline, making the stitches even in size. Work the short stalk next and then the two leaves, each with a central vein leading into the apple stalk. Finish each line of Chain stitches as described for Detached Chain stitch, Fig 5, page 42.

The motif can be repeated on other mats to make a set, or you may wish to extend the idea by working several motifs around a tablecloth, using the single apple on napkins.

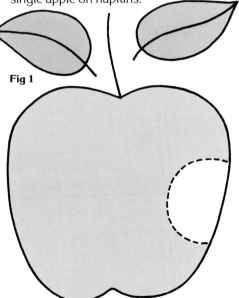

Fig 1

Fig 1 *Trace the apple shape on the solid line for the Apple place mat. Trace the leaves. For Eve's Apple cloth, trace the apple with the bite out of it.*

Eve's apple cloth

The same apple motif is used on the green-checked cloth pictured on the previous page but this time Chain stitches have been used to fill the area, with rows of stitches worked close together.

The fabric for the cloth is, in fact, a dishtowel, which you can buy already hemmed. Embroidered with bright apples, the towel makes a cloth for a small table or a tray cloth.

You can use the same templates that you made for the place mat, but cut a 'bite' from the apple, following the dotted line on the pattern Fig 1, page 40.

Materials required

Green and white checked dishtowel
1 skein each Anchor Pearl cotton No. 5
    as follows: 333 red, 225 and 254 green
Thin cardboard for a template
Crewel needle, size 5

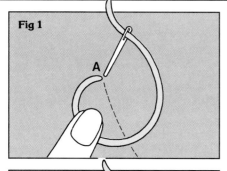
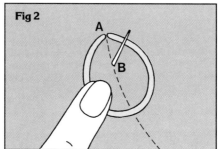
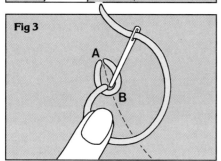
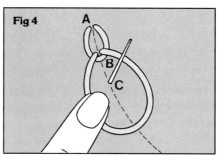

Chain stitch

Chain stitch is an interesting and absorbing stitch to work but it does take time to learn how to get the loops gently curved and of even size. Practise with soft embroidery cotton on a piece of medium-weight fabric – or even a clean dishtowel – until you can work a perfectly formed line of stitches.
1. Bring the needle through at A and, while holding the thread down with the thumb (see Fig 1), insert the needle into the same hole at A (Fig 1).
2. Bring the needle through at B, a short distance in front of A, and coming up through the loop of thread (see Fig 2). The thumb still holds the thread down.
3. As the needle is pulled through, the thread tightens and the chain begins to be formed. When the chain is properly formed, re-insert the needle into the same hole, B, the thumb holding the thread down for the next chain (Fig 3).
4. Bring the needle through at C, the same distance as A–B in front of B (Fig 4).

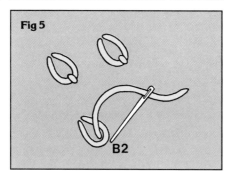

Re-insert the needle into C to form the next chain, the thumb still holding down the loop of thread exactly as in Fig 3. This procedure will form a continuous line of Chain stitches.
5. For a Detached Chain stitch, refer back to Fig 2, bringing the thread through at B. Pull the thread through to form the loop, then insert the needle at B2, outside the loop. This makes a tying stitch which holds the loop secure (Fig 5). This stitch is also used to finish off a continuous row of Chain Stitches.

Preparation

Make the template using the thin cardboard as described for the apple place mat (page 40) and draw the apple and leaves onto each corner of the dishtowel.

The apple can have the 'bite' facing the same direction in all four corners, or you can reverse the template so that the 'bite' is on the other side of the apple.

You will find it easier to work the motifs if the fabric is stretched and held taut in an embroidery hoop and, if filled shapes of solid stitchery are worked without a hoop, there is a risk of your pulling the stitching too tightly, causing the flatness of the fabric to become distorted.

Using the red thread and referring to the Chain stitch diagrams.
stitch round the apple shape on the design outline. When you arrive back at the starting point, continue working Chain stitches along the inside of the previous line of Chain stitches, and work as close to this as possible.

Continue working round inside the apple shape with this continuous line of Chain stitches until it is completely filled.

Work a single line of Chain stitches for the stalk, using the lighter green thread. Use the same shade to work the centre vein of each leaf, and then fill in the upper halves of the leaves. Use the darker green shade to fill the lower half.

You will find the easiest method of filling in each half leaf shape is to work from the stalk end to the tip along the drawn outer line, and then work filling lines of stitches on the inside so that you are working in towards the stitched vein line.

Happy apple suit

The child's shirt and play trousers pictured were purchased separately but, by decorating the garments with embroidery, a charming, co-ordinated outfit is achieved.

Materials required

Purchased play trousers and short-sleeved shirt with collar
Dressmaker's carbon paper
Thin card for a template
Anchor stranded embroidery cotton as follows: 1 skein each of 333 red, 225 emerald and 264 pale olive
Crewel needle, size 7

Preparation

Trace the small apple motif and the tiny leaf spray (Fig 1).

Trace the apple with the bite out of it from Fig 1 page 40.

Make a card template for the larger apple.

Trace the small apple onto one of the shirt's collar points using dressmaker's carbon paper. Reverse the tracing for the apple on the other collar point, so that they are symmetrical. Transfer five leaf sprays around the collar, spacing them equidistantly (see picture).

Using the template draw round the shape on the bib of the play trousers, adding two leaves and a stalk. Using dressmaker's carbon paper, transfer leaf sprays to the straps of the play trousers (see picture).

Working the embroidery

Shirt Work the shirt first, holding the garment freely in the hand for embroidery.

Using three strands of thread throughout, work the small apples in red thread using Chain stitches (see opposite). The stitches are very small for this project (see detail). Work the outlines first, then fill in with stitches, working round inside the shape.

Using the darker green thread, work the apple stalk with about six Chain stitches.

The leaves are single, larger Chain stitches, set either side of the stalk. When working these, it is important not to pull the thread too tightly, as this will produce a thin-looking leaf. If the thread

is allowed to loop naturally, a gently-curved leaf shape will appear.

Work the leaf sprays round the collar in the same way.

Play trousers The leaf sprays on the straps can be worked freely in the hand but a hoop is advised for working the large apple on the bib, as this will prevent the fabric puckering while you are working the massed area of stitchery. If however, a hoop is not available, you must be very careful with your work to see that the tension of the stitches is even throughout.

Fig 1 *Trace the small apple and leaf spray for the Happy Apple playsuit*

Embroider the apple with Chain stitches, following the same method described for Eve's apple cloth. The stalk is a single row of Chain stitches and the two leaves are worked using both shades of green (see detail).

For a finishing touch, sew matching red buttons to the shirt and the bib of the play trousers.

Forget-me-not table linen

In this Chain stitch project, the design uses lines of Chain stitches for the flower stems, with single or detached Chain stitches for the small leaves. Groups of detached Chain stitches make the forget-me-not flower heads and when used in this way they are called Lazy Daisy stitches.

This is an opportunity for you to use your own sense of creativity in embroidery by positioning the flower heads and tiny leaves where you would like to see them.

Materials required

For a 150cm (60in)-square tablecloth and 4 napkins (purchased)
DMC Coton Perlé No. 5 as follows: 1 skein of white; 2 skeins of 743 and 742 yellows; 4 skeins each of 955, 369 and 913 greens; 4 skeins each of 747, 813 and 800 blues
Tracing paper
Coloured crayons
Crewel needle, size 7

Preparation

Trace the pattern (Fig 1, page 46). Spread the tracing on a flat surface and place each of the napkins on top, in turn. Trace the design using a fabric transfer pencil.

Trace the posy of flowers onto the corners of the tablecloth and then re-position the cloth to trace a complete border of the intertwined design lines, linking the posies. The areas of the border between arrows are repeated to the length of border required.

Lazy Daisies

Lazy Daisy stitches are worked in a circular formation, the stitches radiating from a central point. The basic stitch is Chain stitch.

For Lazy Daisy stitch, the needle is re-inserted in the same central hole to begin each petal (Fig 1).

The stitch can also be used so that the knots are towards the middle of the flower and this produces a pointed rather than a rounded petal (Fig 2).

Fig 1

Fig 2

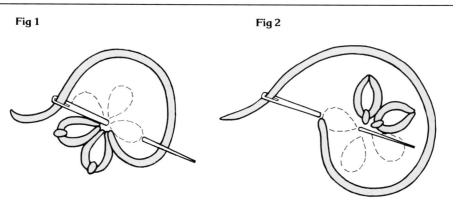

Working the embroidery

A 20cm *(8in)* -diameter embroidery hoop is recommended for working the tablecloth and napkins, as this will prevent the fabric puckering and make the stitching easier.

Using each of the three shades of green thread, work the posy stems. Balance the use of each colour to please yourself. Scatter a few Detached Chain stitches along the stems to represent small leaves.

Work the intertwined lines which form the border and, using the paler greens, scatter small Detached Chain stitched leaves along them at intervals. Refer to page 42, Fig 5 for Detached Chain stitches.

Work the clusters of forget-me-not flowers around the stem heads using the three blue shades of thread (see picture).

Scatter flowers randomly along the intertwined lines. Finish each flower with a small Detached Chain stitch in its centre, using one of the yellow threads.

To finish, cut two lengths of the white Coton Perlé, each measuring 15cm *(6in)* long and, threading the lengths into the needle, weave them through the Chain stitches, down one side of the embroidered stalks of each posy and up the other so that the two loose ends are on the right side of the fabric. Then tie the ends into a small neat bow (see picture).

Work the tablecloth posies and intertwined border in the same way.

Fig 1 *Trace-off pattern for the Forget-me-not table napkin. Trace the flower spray separately for the tablecloth corners, then repeat the sections of intertwined border between arrows for the tablecloth border*

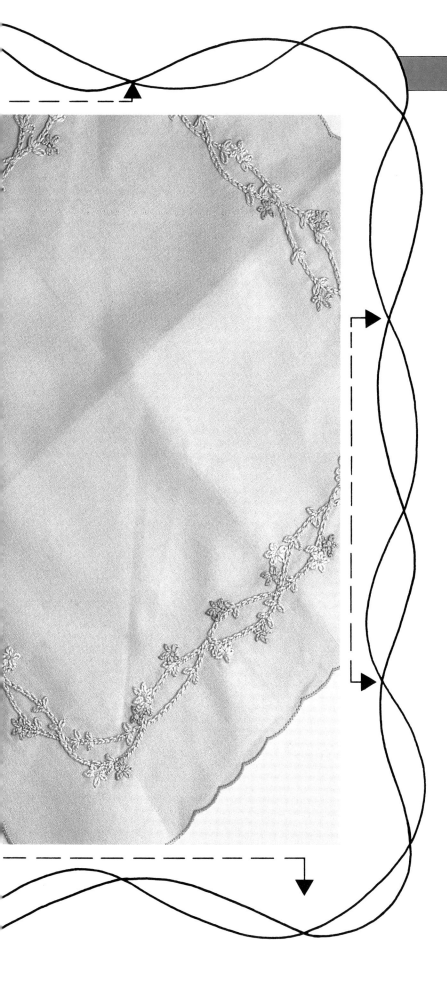

Ideas for flower motifs

Flower sprays have many applications in embroidery, both for home items and for garments and accessories. The corner spray on the Forget-me-not table linen has been worked entirely in Chain stitches but, if you prefer, other stitches could be used instead – such as Satin stitch, French knots and Stem stitch.

The motif would look charming on bed linens, perhaps on the corner of the top sheet and on the pillow cases, worked white on white, or white on pastel colours.

It could also be used on the four corners of a cushion, or be worked on guest towels. Worked in a range of bright pastel shades, the spray makes a pretty picture perhaps framed with an oval mount.

In fashion, try the motif on a blouse or dress front, or on the ends of a silky scarf and it is the ideal size for embroidering on lingerie or night wear. Repeated and linked with the ribbon border, the spray would also look pretty around the hem of a long baby gown.

Buttonhole Stitch

There is no real difference between Buttonhole stitch and Blanket stitch. The former is worked so that the stitches lie close together and the latter has stitches spaced evenly apart. Both variations are in this chapter, where you are given an appliqué motif for bathroom towels, ideas for decorating table linen with motifs abstracted from a teaset, and a pretty camisole top to make with cutwork decoration.

Appliquéd bathroom towel

The technique used to decorate the towel pictured is called 'appliqué'. This is where a motif is applied with stitches to the background fabric.

This popular – and easy– embroidery technique has many applications, from children's clothes to high fashion, and from small room accessories to larger items like bed covers, quilts and curtains.

Blanket stitch has been used here to apply the motifs but Buttonhole stitch and machine-worked Satin stitch are both used for appliqué, depending on the item being made.

Before starting an appliqué project, make sure that both the background fabric and the appliqué fabric are colourfast and have been pre-shrunk. If you are not sure, wash them both.

Materials required
To apply 1 motif to a towel
Plain white towel
15cm *(6in)* square of lavender blue cotton fabric
15cm *(6in)* square of pale green cotton fabric
Anchor stranded embroidery cotton as follows: 1 skein each of 130 blue, 241 pale jade green, 01 white, 06 peach
Basting thread
Crewel needle, size 7
15 × 30cm *(6 × 12in)* piece of lightweight iron-on interfacing

Note: if you are decorating a set of towels, bathtowels or handtowels, you will need additional fabric and interfacing and, possibly, extra embroidery thread.

Buttonhole stitch

Both Buttonhole stitch and Blanket stitch are worked from left to right and success depends on keeping the stitches upright and even in length.
1. Bring the needle through on the bottom design line A. Insert the needle at B on the top design line and slightly to the right (Fig 1). Bring the needle out at C directly below B. Before pulling the needle through, take the thread under the needle point.
2. Pull the needle through to form the stitch. Insert the needle at D on the top design line and bring it out at E, immediately below, with the thread under

the needle point as shown in Fig 2.
3. Pull the needle and thread through and then continue to make stitches in the same way, very close together (Fig 3).
4. Blanket stitch is worked in exactly the same way but stitches are spaced equidistantly apart (Fig 4).

You may find it difficult at first to make this stitch successfully because it is all too easy to pull the thread too tightly and so fail to get a 'right-angled' stitch. Practice is important to achieve the right tension and, while you are practising, try out stitches of different lengths and with different spacings. You will be interested to see how many variations can be achieved with a single stitch.

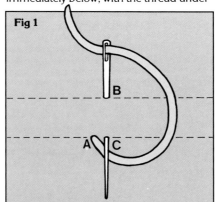

Fig 1

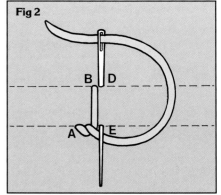

Fig 2

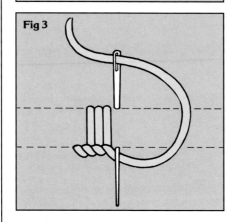

Fig 3

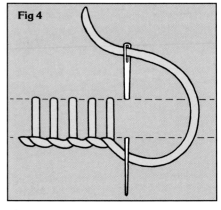

Fig 4

Preparation

Trace the flower and leaf shapes from Fig 1 onto paper and cut out on the solid lines to make paper patterns. Pin the patterns to the fabrics and cut out one flower from the blue fabric and two leaves from the green fabric. (Repeat this if you are cutting out more flowers.)

Trace the broken line on your paper patterns from Fig 1. Cut out on the broken line. Use the patterns to cut shapes from iron-on interfacing (making sure that the adhesive side of the interfacing is uppermost). Again, cut one flower and two leaf shapes.

Following the manufacturer's instructions, press the interfacing shapes to the wrong side of the fabric shapes, centring them.

Using a pair of small, sharply-pointed scissors, snip into the edge of each shape towards the interfacing. The cuts enable you to fold the small turning neatly onto the wrong side. Work basting stitches to hold the turning (Fig 2).

Arrange the flower and leaves on one corner of the towel with the flower overlapping the leaves slightly (see picture).

Pin and then baste the shapes to the towel.

Working the embroidery

The embroidery can be worked freely in the hand without the use of a hoop.

Using three strands of embroidery cotton, work Blanket stitches (see Fig 4, page 48) around the flower and leaf edges. Try and make each stitch 3mm (¹/₈in) in length and space them 3mm (¹/₈in) apart – but if stitches are longer than this and wider apart it does not matter as long as they are regular and even. Where the flower overlaps the leaves there is extra thickness of fabric and extra care must be taken with stitchery at this point.

When the shapes are applied, remove the basting stitches.

Using green thread, work lines on the leaves using either Back stitch (page 37) or Chain stitch (page 42).

Using peach thread and Back stitch, work radiating lines from the centre of the flower (Fig 1). Work a single small detached Chain stitch (page 42) in white at the end of each line.

When working embroidery stitches on appliqué, remember that you do not

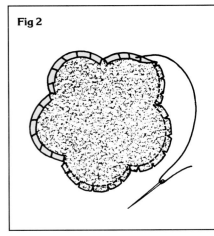

Fig 2 *Preparing appliqué: snip into the edges and turn to the wrong side. Baste to hold the turning*

have to take stitching through the towel as the motifs are already firmly attached with Blanket stitching. Work the stitches through the surface layer of fabric only.

Finishing

The towel pictured has a woven border running across the towel and this has been edged with Blanket stitches in green thread for a finishing touch.

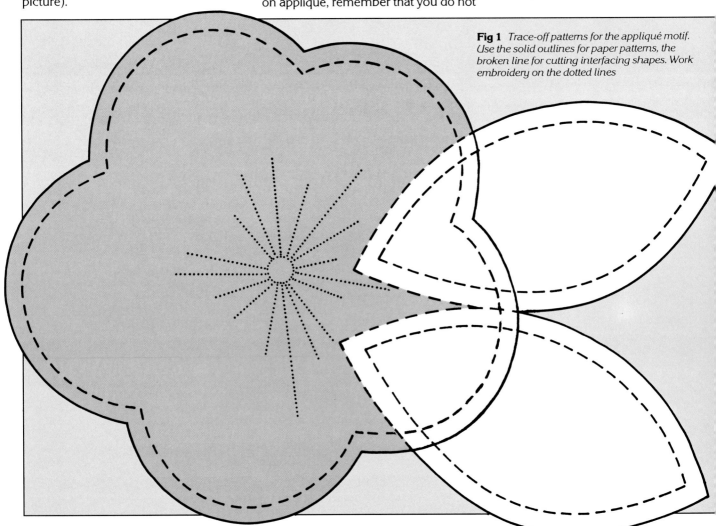

Fig 1 *Trace-off patterns for the appliqué motif. Use the solid outlines for paper patterns, the broken line for cutting interfacing shapes. Work embroidery on the dotted lines*

Camisole with cutwork

Buttonhole stitch is used for the type of embroidery called 'cutwork'. In this technique, areas of the pattern are bordered with Buttonhole stitches and the background fabric is cut away. Traditionally, cutwork was worked on white fabric with white embroidery but modern cutwork often has pretty, colourful effects, as can be seen in the camisole pictured.

The camisole was made from a commercial paper pattern, using a finely woven cotton fabric with a woven satin dot.

Materials required

Plain white camisole top with a scooped neckline
DMC stranded embroidery cotton as follows: 1 skein each of 819 pale pink, 775 pale blue, 369 pale green
Crewel needle size 7
Pale blue satin ribbon 3mm *(⅛in)* wide for straps (optional)
Matching coloured crayons

Preparation

Measure and mark the centre of the neckline with basting stitches.

Trace the design (Fig 1) directly onto the fabric using sharply-pointed crayons in colours close to the embroidery threads. Position the motif about 15mm *(⅝in)* below the neckline edge.

Working the embroidery

The embroidery is worked freely in the hand.

Using three strands of embroidery thread throughout, work Buttonhole stitch (page 48) on all the design lines, referring to the picture. Work all the stitches so that the knots lie on the solid lines of the design. Use the broken line as a guide to the length of the stitch.

Work the flowers in pale pink, the leaves and flower centres in pale green and the triangle in pale blue.

Working cutwork

With a very sharp pair of pointed scissors, cut away the fabric areas which are shown as blue on Fig 1. The edges must be smooth and neat but care must be taken to see that the

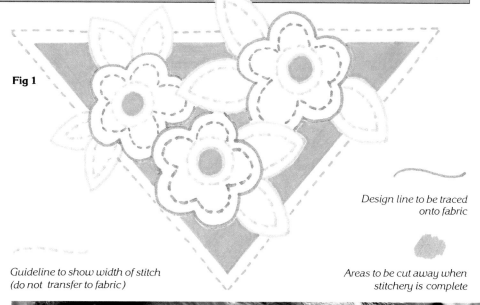

Fig 1

Design line to be traced onto fabric

Guideline to show width of stitch (do not transfer to fabric)

Areas to be cut away when stitchery is complete

stitches are not cut.

You will find it easier to cut away a shape if you pierce the blade of the scissors into the middle of the area and then, very carefully, cut towards the line of Buttonhole stitches. Cut close to the stitches but do not damage them.

When all the work has been

completed, press the camisole gently on the wrong side to make the stitching stand out.

Finishing

If desired, the camisole can be given straps of pale blue satin ribbon, finished with tiny stitched bows.

Fig 1 *Trace the design from the chinaware and simplify the lines and shapes*

Fig 2 *The design is simplified even further for working in appliqué and embroidery*

Embroidery patterns from chinaware

Inspiration for embroidery designs are to be found all about you, but one of the most obvious sources of potential embroidery motifs lies in furnishing fabrics, wallpapers and one's own chinaware.

The tray mat and napkin in the picture have an appliqué and embroidery design on them which has been abstracted from a teaset. Co-ordinated china and table linen has considerable eye-appeal and makes a good conversation point.

Designing from china

If some of the areas of design are going to be interpreted into appliqué, they need to be simplified. Fig 1 shows the design of the china pattern pictured and Fig 2 shows it simplified for appliqué. When translated into thread, the larger flowers are appliquéd with Buttonhole stitch while the remaining, smaller flowers and leaves are worked in detached Chain stitches, Straight stitches, Back stitches and French knots.

Select a fairly large plate from the set of china and trace the design as carefully as possible. Spread your tracing out before you and study it.

You will probably feel the line is rather shaky and in need of 'tidying up'. Do this by redrawing or tracing over the shapes, smoothing lines and possibly simplifying some areas in order to make it more suitable for stitchery.

Rearrange the motifs into the shape required to fit the table linen. For example, you may wish to straighten the curved border of a plate so that it will fit along the straight edge of a tray cloth – as has been done with the tea set border.

Next, decide which areas are to be appliquéd and then decide how you can best interpret the rest of the design.

You can always practise your stitches on a small scrap of fabric – even an old handkerchief – in order to choose which stitches look best.

Once you have decided how to work the design, prepare the appliqué shapes. In this project the shapes are prepared in a different way to that of the appliqué towel project (page 48), where the raw edges of shapes were turned to the wrong side and then evenly-shaped Blanket stitches were used to attach the motif to the towel.

Preparing for appliqué

Cut out the paper patterns without a turning allowance. Bond the fabrics to the iron-on interfacing. Using the paper patterns, cut out the motifs, with no allowance for turnings.

Pin the fabric shapes in position on the table linen, carefully re-arranging and adjusting until you are satisfied that they are correctly placed. Use the original tracing of the design to help you, by placing it over the arrangement and adjusting the appliqué shapes as necessary underneath.

Pin, then baste the shapes in place.

Using three strands of embroidery cotton, work a neat line of Buttonhole stitch (page 48, Fig 1–Fig 3) around each shape so that the knots of the stitches lie on the outer edge of each shape, with the 'arms' of the stitches closely protecting the raw edge of the appliqué shape (Fig 3 this page).

The line of Buttonhole stitching should look smooth and be of even tension.

Work around all the appliqué shapes and then, using different coloured threads and the most appropriate stitch, work the remaining areas of embroidery.

As you can see from the picture, in the example of embroidery worked, stitches, threads and fabrics have been thoughtfully chosen, as the design has simple shapes.

The stems and small flower centres are worked in a deep rose colour, the stems being interpreted in Back stitch (see page 37) and small French knots.

The blue petals of the small flowers are detached Chain stitches or Lazy Daisy stitches (see page 44).

The leaves are worked in two shades of moss green in long Straight stitches (see page 10) to fill in the leaf shape and gave an effect of shading which closely follows the design on the china.

When all the stitchery is completed, press the table linen gently on the wrong side to encourage the stitchery to stand out on the right side.

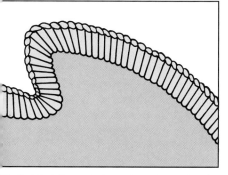

Fig 3 *Work Buttonhole stitch on the appliqué edges, so that the knots lie on the outer edge*

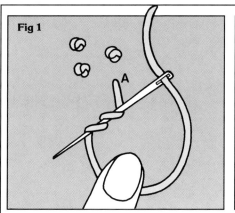

French knots

French knots can be used singly as spots in a design and are often used for the stamens of flowers.

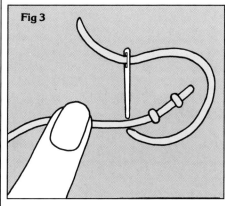

1. Bring the needle through at A (where the knot is desired) and wind the thread round the needle twice as shown (Fig 1).
2. Holding the thread down with the thumb, twist the needle back to A and insert if where it first came out (Fig 2). Holding the knot down with the thumb, pull the thread through from the back and secure the knot on the wrong side.

Couching

A thread is laid along the fabric surface and held down while a different needle and thread works small holding stitches over it at intervals (Fig 3).

Mixed Stitches

With the stitches you have learned so far, a whole new world of embroidery opens up before you and, as your expertise grows, so will your confidence in undertaking more complicated pieces. In this chapter, there is a cushion to work in crewel wools, a miniature picture to embroider, a Persian patterned scarf and some ideas for making a needlework 'portrait' of your home. Finally, there are ideas for 'scribbling' on a T-shirt.

Crewel-work cushion

Crewel embroidery is the name given to a free-flowing style of design (usually floral), worked in two-ply lightly twisted wool on linen, twill or satinised cotton fabric. A variety of stitches are traditionally used in crewel work, and shading with Long and Short stitches is one of the features of the embroidery.

The cushion pictured is a modern interpretation of crewel work (sometimes called Jacobean embroidery).

Materials required
Size: 35cm *(14in)*-square cushion
45 × 90cm *(18 × 36in)* piece of satinised embroidery fabric in a natural shade
Paterna Persian yarn as follows: 2 skeins each of 923, 924, 925 wood rose, 513, 514, 515 old blue, 523, 524, 525 teal blue
Chenille needle size 18
Cushion pad

Preparation
Cut the fabric into two pieces, each 45cm *(18in)* square. Put one aside for the cushion back.

Enlarge the design (Fig 1) photo-graphically to 28cm *(11in)* across. Trace the photographic print and draw over the lines on the wrong side with an embroidery transfer pencil. Following the manufacturer's instructions, transfer the design to the fabric.

Alternatively, trace the design onto the fabric using dressmaker's carbon paper.

Working the embroidery
The detail shows the way in which the

Fig 1

Fig 1 *Pattern for the crewel-work cushion. Enlarge this photographically and then trace for a pattern*

colour shading has been worked on the flowers and leaves. Long and Short stitches (see page 20) are worked to achieve this effect and the length of the stitches can be adjusted to fit a shape.

Begin with the darker yarn shades and work towards the edges of shapes using the medium tone and then the lightest colour. The large flower has petals shaded in the pink yarns, with

Buttonhole stitch (page 48) petals in the centre worked in old blue shades.

Detached Chain stitches (page 42) in dark pink are worked in the centre of each blue petal.

The smaller flowers are worked in old blue yarns, the darker shade towards the middle of each petal, with the lighter shades at the outside edges of the flower. French knots (page 53) in dark pink are grouped in the centres.

The stems and inner leaves are worked in Stem stitch (below) using the medium leaf yarn. The leaves are shaded in the three leaf yarns.

The smaller leaves are worked with Long and Short stitches in the light leaf yarn on one side and outlined with a darker tone on the other. Small French knots in the darker shade are worked in a row to represent the leaf vein.

To add texture to the embroidery, a leaf stem and the stem of the large flower have been further embellished by needle-weaving a lighter leaf thread through the stitchery.

Making the cushion
Do not press wool embroidery, as this may flatten the stitches.

Trim the embroidered fabric back to 38cm (15in)-square, keeping the embroidery centred. Trim the cushion back to the same size.

Place the front and back together right sides facing. Pin and baste on three sides. Machine-stitch taking a 12mm (½in) seam. Trim the corners diagonally and turn to the right side.

Insert the cushion pad and close the open seam with hand-sewing.

Finishing
Twist a cord from the remaining blue yarns and sew it round the cushion, tying the ends in a knot at one corner. Fringe the knot ends. (Refer to page 9 for the technique of making cords).

Persian-patterned scarf

The rich colours and flowing floral design worked on this wool scarf were inspired by the pattern of an old Persian embroidery. Here the border pattern is worked on two sides of a square but it could be repeated to go on all four sides if desired.

The scale of the design makes it suitable for larger items also, such as a bed cover or a room divider curtain.

Fig 1 (page 58) is the corner motif which could be repeated round the sides of a square or rectangle. Fig 2 is a finishing motif such as that used for the ends of the border on the scarf.

Materials required
Finished size 60cm (24in) square
60cm (24in) square of finely woven wool fabric
Fabric transfer pencil
DMC Laine Medicis as follows: 1 skein each of 8103 red, 8129 salmon, 8139 light salmon, 8505A very pale salmon, 8328 very pale yellow, 8327 mustard yellow, 8402 grass green, 8415 dark green
Tapestry needle, size 20
Turquoise sewing thread (optional)

Preparation
Trace the pattern from Fig 1 and Fig 2 (pages 58–59) to make a border and then draw over the lines on the wrong side of the tracing with a fabric transfer pencil.

Following the manufacturer's instructions, transfer the design onto the fabric so that it is positioned along two adjoining sides.

Working the embroidery
An embroidery hoop should be used for working this project.

Use three strands of wool together throughout.

Work the stems of the trailing plants in Stem stitch (left) using grass green yarn.

Work the inner leaves in the darker green and the other leaves in grass green using Long and Short stitches (page 20).

The flowers are worked in Long and Short stitches (page 20), each using three different colours and you may use your own creativity in deciding what these colours should be.

Stem stitch

1. Bring the thread through on the design line at A and hold it down with the thumb as shown in Fig 1. Insert the needle at B and bring it out at C, halfway between A and B.

Pull the needle and thread through to set the first stitch. Holding the thread down with the thumb (see Fig 2) insert the needle at D (exactly the same distance as A–C from where the thread emerges) and bring it out at B.

3. Insert the needle at E and bring it out at D (Fig 3). Continue making stitches in this way.

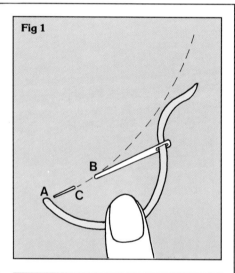

Fig 1

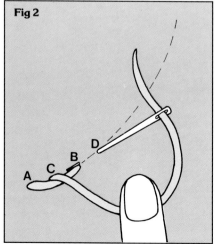

Fig 2

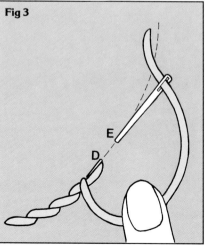

Fig 3

Finishing

To finish the scarf with a fringe, either work a row of machine-stitching using matching sewing thread 4cm *(1¹/₂in)* from the raw edge, or work a row of Back stitches (page 37) in mustard yellow yarn. Pull threads from the fabric edge to make a 4cm *(1¹/₂in)* fringe.

Ideas for the motif

The flower spray in the Persian pattern design is fairly open and can therefore be used for different embroidery techniques. For instance, it could be used as a quilting pattern for a purse or belt, or for a long padded waistcoat.

The design might also be worked in outline stitches for table linens – try the effects of outlining the pattern in Stem stitch or Back stitch, worked as a border on a tablecloth.

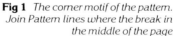

Fig 1 *The corner motif of the pattern. Join Pattern lines where the break in the middle of the page*

Fly stitch

Bring the needle through at A, insert it at B and bring it out again at C. Work a couching stitch over the loop to hold it and then take the needle to the next position for another Fly stitch.

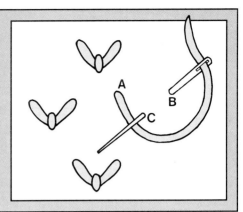

The Persian border is designed to be worked on two sides of a small scarf, using the Fig 1 corner and the Fig 2 end motif. It can be extended to any length, for a shawl, or can be worked on all four edges of a larger piece, such as a quilt or curtain.

Fig 2 *Use this motif at the ends of the Fig 1 corner motif to complete the scarf design*

Miniature in embroidery

This small embroidered picture is the first project where you begin to use a wide variety of the stitches with which you are now familiar. You will see how their different shapes can be used together to give different effects and how these in turn can be used to build up a simple but beautiful image.

Again, the use of fabric transfer crayons gives the background colour on which to build the areas of stitchery.

The idea for this project came from looking at a view of gardens photographed as colour transparencies.

A fabric frame shaped like a transparency mount would be an attractive and unusual way of displaying this type of embroidery picture. Cut a frame shape from pelmet-weight interfacing and cover it with fabric in a complementary colour. Glue the finished embroidery behind the frame. Sew on a small ring for hanging.

Materials required
25 × 50cm *(10 × 20in)* piece of white polycotton fabric
DMC stranded embroidery cotton as follows: 1 skein each of 702 mid green, 954 pale jade, 955 very pale jade, 809 pale blue, 775 very pale blue, 211 pale mauve, 402 rust, 754 salmon
Crewel needle, size 7
1 packet fabric transfer crayons

Preparation
Place a piece of tracing paper over the picture and trace off the general outlines. Very lightly crayon in the areas as evenly as possible. Do not press hard, as this gives very strong colours and the effect you want to achieve is one of light, delicate shading.

Fold the piece of white polycotton in half to give a double layer measuring 25 × 25cm *(10 × 10in)*. Iron the folded fabric to remove any creases.

Transfer the crayonned design onto the fabric, following the manufacturer's instructions.

Place the doubled layer of fabric into a wooden embroidery hoop 20cm *(8in)* in diameter, stretching the fabric to achieve a taut area within the hoop.

Working the embroidery
Use three strands of embroidery cotton throughout the stitchery.

Work the outer arch in two rows of the darker rust shade and one row of the paler rust shade using Back stitch (page 38).

Work the inner arch in one row of the darker rust and one row in paler rust, side by side, again in Back stitch.

The gate is also worked in Back stitch, using the darker rust shade throughout, working three lines of stitches close to one another for each gate post and then single lines for the cross bars.

Using the two paler shades of green, work small groups of Detached Chain stitches (see page 42) along the outer arch to represent small clumps of leaves.

Using the two deeper shades of green, work the leaves in clumps around the inner arch.

Using only the very pale green, scatter tiny Detached Chain stitches all over the lightly-coloured hedge archway. The tiny stitches should be made so that they face in all directions to form a random covering of surface texture.

Using the three shades of green thread, work the small clumps of foliage in the foreground in Back stitch. Work groups of mauve and blue Detached Chain stitches so that they look like tiny flowers.

Finally, around the outer arch, scatter a few tiny light blue, Detached Chain stitches and then a few deeper blue Chain stitches (page 42) around the inner arch.

throughout except when outlining the face, hands and eyes (398 grey) and the mouth (29 red), where only one strand is used.

The striped dress is worked in lines of Chain stitch (page 42) and Stem stitch. The outlining is done in Chain stitch.

The apron has a Chain-stitched waistband with a Blanket stitch outline. Work the spots in Straight stitches worked side by side and touching (Satin stitch and outline the blue

spots with Stem stitch.

The legs and boots are outlined in Stem stitch and the spots on the stockings are French knots (page 53), as are the eyes. Work the boots in brown wool Straight stitches (page 10) and work Cross stitches (page 22) for the laces. The smiling mouth is worked in Stem stitch.

Far left *The colour drawing by Cluny Johnstone from which the embroidery was worked*

Portrait of Mummy

Children's drawings make the most marvellous designs for embroidered pictures because they are usually simple in line, and colour is massed in large areas.

If you are using this book to teach young children embroidery, you might encourage them to embroider their own pictures, as a way of stimulating enthusiasm.

Embroidered pictures of family and friends make very acceptable gifts for special occasions and a child could perhaps include the recipients' hobby or special interest – gardening or cooking, for example – in the portrait.

'Portrait of Mummy' was designed by 3 year-old Cluny Johnstone, and embroidered by her grandmother. The embroidery is reproduced actual size.

Materials used
35 × 25cm *(14 × 10in)* piece of old sheeting fabric
35 × 25cm *(14 × 10in)* piece of light-weight iron-on interfacing
Anchor stranded embroidery cotton as follows: 1 skein each of 410 blue, 238 green; small amount of 29 red, 398 grey
Brown darning wool
Crewel needle, size 7

Preparation
Iron the fabric onto the interfacing.
Transfer the drawing to the fabric using dressmaker's carbon or embroidery transfer pencil.

Working the embroidery
Use two strands of embroidery thread

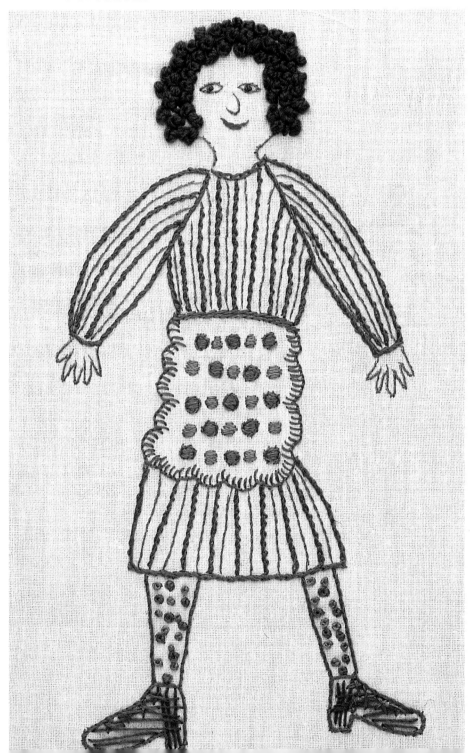

Jane's window

This embroidered picture is worked with a combination of fabric dye crayons and free surface stitchery. Several stitches have been used to give the various effects – leaves, flowers, brickwork and louvred window shutters – and this type of picture presents an opportunity for trying out all the stitches you have learned in this book.

Perhaps it will give you ideas for your own embroidery design of a 'portrait' of your house or apartment.

Materials required

38 × 75cm *(15 × 30in)* piece of white cotton fabric
Wooden frame approximately 35cm *(14in)* square.
Madeira stranded embroidery floss as follows: 1 skein each of M3328 russet pink, M352 salmon, M351 orange, M602 bright pink, M798 mid-blue, M906 bright green, M955 pale jade, M913 mid-jade, M943 emerald, M911 bright jade
Crewel needle, size 7
1 packet of fabric dye crayons
Piece of cardboard 28 × 31cm *(11 × 12½in)*
Fine string or buttonhole thread
A large sheet of tracing paper

Preparation

Fold the fabric in half to give a stronger and firmer double layer measuring 38cm *(15in)* square.

Place the tracing paper over the picture on this page and trace it, using the fabric dye crayons to draw and colour in the window and brickwork design. Take care not to smudge the waxy crayons, as this will give a blurred effect on the finished fabric.

Transfer the tracing onto the doubled fabric, following the manufacturer's instructions.

Stretch the doubled fabric over the frame.

Working the embroidery

The brickwork lines are embroidered in three strands of M3328 in rows of Running stitch. The shaded bricks are then worked over in several Cross stitches using three strands of M352.

The bright pink and red geraniums (M351 and M602) are worked with six strands of thread in small clusters of Detached Chain stitch which are placed very closely together so that they give a rich and massed effect.

The small blue flowers (M798) are worked in six strands of thread and are formed by working two or three French knots for each flower to give a richly raised effect.

The small salmon-coloured flowers are similarly worked in six strands as tiny Cross stitches, using M352.

The window shutters are worked in six strands of mid-jade (M913). The louvre pattern is created by working lines of Blanket stitch across each shutter which is then outlined in Back stitch.

Back stitch, in three strands of thread (M955), is also used to outline the upper half of the window, which appears as a pale green blind, and then similarly in darker green (M913) for the lower half of the window.

Using this same green thread, work a scalloped line of Blanket stitch across the lower edge of the window blind, varying the size of the Blanket stitches to create the scallop shapes. From the centre point of this edge, work a short line of Chain stitches and then a small circlet of Blanket stitches to represent the cord of the blind.

The same green thread is also used to work the tiny Straight stitch stalks of the flowers which decorate the blind.

Work the flowers of the blind in M352, using six strands together, working three small Straight stitches radiating outwards from each stalk.

Work the stems of the geraniums in M906, using six strands together and working small, even Back stitches.

Similarly, work the grassy leaves in M911 in curved lines of Back stitches to give a spiked effect.

The geranium leaves are worked with three strands of thread, using M943 and M911 as appropriate, working circles of Blanket stitch to give the full and rounded shapes that are required.

Finally, the sprigs of tiny leaves are worked by building up small groups of Detached Chain stitches in M906 and M943, encircling the blue and salmon flowers and then trailing downwards so that they appear to be growing from the window box.

When the stitchery is complete, remove the fabric from the frame. Stretch the fabric, lacing it over the card. The picture is now ready for framing.

House 'portrait'

Whether you live in a small, individual town house, a country cottage, a house in a row or in an apartment, you can probably work a charming 'portrait' of your home in embroidery. Take a photograph as straight-on as you can and have it enlarged to a workable size. Trace and re-trace the picture, simplifying fussy details and perhaps even removing unsightly features, such as down pipes. Emphasise those features which you think give your home character – perhaps an unusual window shape, or decorative roof details. When the design seems pleasing, trace it onto fabric and colour with crayons before planning the embroidery.

Scribble on a T-shirt

You can embroider a T-shirt with lines and swirls of embroidery for a distinctive fashion look using just one stitch – Chain stitch, the stitches massed in rows for a bold effect.

Use soft embroidery cotton or Pearl cotton and a crewel needle, size 7.

Cotton jersey tends to stretch during working and you may find it helps to work over a pillow. Pin brown paper round the pillow closely and slip the T-shirt onto it, so that the fabric is supported.

Sketch design lines with a piece of chalk or crayon (or wear the T-shirt and get a friend to scribble on you!).

Key to embroidery

A   Three single rows of Chain stitch in orange, green and mauve

B   Four rows of Chain stitch in purple, three rows in green, and two rows in orange

C   Four lines of Chain stitch crossed, each line with three rows in blue, pink, mauve and green

D   Lines of three rows in Chain stitch, with Buttonhole-stitched edging in mauve and green

E   Three single curved rows of Chain stitch in green, mauve and orange

F   Three lines of Chain stitch crossed, each line with two rows, in blue, pink and purple

G   Three rows of Chain stitch worked in a spiral with two rows superimposed on the third in a twisted line, in gold, purple and mauve. A bow is sewn on the end of the line.

H   Three lines of two rows of Chain stitch with one row of Buttonhole stitch worked over, in purple, pink/gold and green/gold

I   Five lines of Chain stitch crossed, each line with two rows of Chain stitch in green, pink, orange and purple. Bows are sewn at the ends of lines.

J   Two curved lines of three rows of Chain stitch, edged with Buttonhole stitch, in blue and orange

K   Lines of Chain stitch with rows twisted over each other in pink, green/gold and mauve

L   Lines of two rows of Chain stitch crossed in pink, blue and purple

PHILIP'S

IN ASSOCIATION WITH

**Royal
Geographical
Society**
with IBG

MODERN
SCHOOL
ATLAS

99th EDITION

KEY STAGE 4, GCSE AND A-LEVEL

SUBJECT LIST

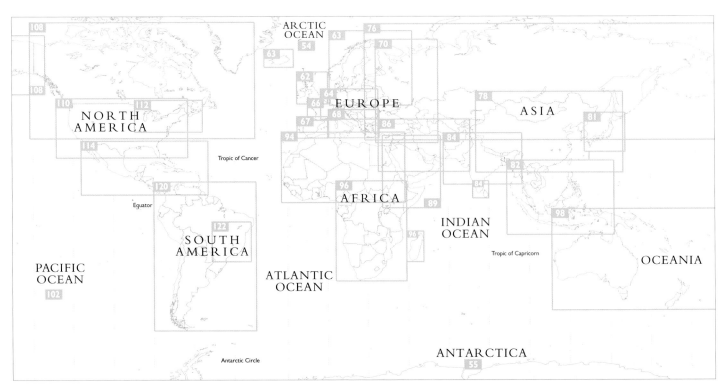

ARCTIC OCEAN

NORTH AMERICA

Tropic of Cancer

Equator

PACIFIC OCEAN

SOUTH AMERICA

ATLANTIC OCEAN

EUROPE

AFRICA

ASIA

INDIAN OCEAN

Tropic of Capricorn

OCEANIA

ANTARCTICA

Antarctic Circle